BIG DOLLAR$ FROM SMALL BUILDINGS

How to Create and Quickly Grow Lifetime Passive Cash Flow with Small Commercial Properties

By F. Scott Tonges

DISCLAIMER

The information in this report is designed to provide accurate & authoritative information regarding the subject matter covered. It is sold with the understanding that the author & publisher are not engaged in rendering legal, accounting, or other professional services to any person. If legal advice and/or other expert assistance is required, the service of a competent professional should be sought.

From the Declaration of Principles jointly adopted by the Committed of the American Bar Association and the Committee of Publishers.

Copyright 2017 By F. Scott Tonges & Cash Cow Books, Inc

All Rights Reserved

"$ 1 Million to Invest"

Some years back a good friend who owns and develops hotels for a living called me to ask if I would help a relative who had one million dollars to invest and wanted to buy a hotel. I was heavily active brokering hotels at the time so jumped at the chance. After a few outings with the client, I asked him, as I often did of successful people I got to know, "How did you pull together the million dollars?"

He told me about his coming to America to take a job with a relative in New York. That opportunity didn't work out, but another relative in the San Francisco bay area had an opening at one of his convenience stores. He owned several. Taking the job on the night shift to start, he worked hard and learned the business. In time, he was put in charge of several stores the relative owned. Saving his money, he eventually bought his first store for himself. Having learned the business, he used that one store to buy more and in time he owned seven convenience stores. Eventually, he sold off four of the stores, keeping the other three for ongoing, passive cash flow. It was from the 4 sales that he got the one million dollars. I've heard similar stories and others like it many times. I could summarize it like this: learn a business, buy a business, expand a business.

This series of steps took him many years. I don't recall exactly, but at least 15 years to go from night shift employee to millionaire with passive, ongoing cash flow. A convenience store is a business, not a true income property, but the same thing he did to parlay his business into increasing cash flow can be done much easier with real estate. **_The question most have is "How did this owner parlay into multiple properties when most owners struggle to buy, then operate just one? What's the secret?_**

This report will reveal how to create money from nothing to become an investor if you're new at it, how to accelerate the development of a portfolio if you're already a real estate investor, and will give you a blueprint to create substantial lifetime, passive cash flow.

Accelerated Passive Cash Flow And Real World Monopoly

Have you ever played Monopoly, the board game? You start with a little cash, then buy some land for which you can charge modest rents and, if all goes well, you buy a few green houses then collect more rent and then, if things go really well, you buy the big red hotels to put on your property and charge even bigger rents. From then on, you're on easy street. You get a big rent payment as other players come and go across your real estate empire. This can be duplicated in real life and in relatively short order, and it's a lot easier to understand than you might think. In the real world, it's possible <u>to start with no money or credit and earn seed capital to invest</u>, <u>buy a first income property</u>, then <u>parlay that one into several</u>, In about 5 years, one could own a passive income portfolio generating $85,000 a year, have $350,000 in the bank, and a net worth from the portfolio of $1.1 million. You can do more in this same time frame if you repeat the first step, earning seed capital, beyond year one. It's not a guarantee, but this report will show you how it's done & other opportunities in real estate investing too. Here's to your success!

F. Scott Tonges / Spring 2017

WIDGETS FOR SALE

I once bought a course about using classified ads to make money. I think the same concept I'll share could be applied today with E-Bay. The premise was, you come up with a specific product idea and advertise it in the "for sale" section as "Widgets for Sale". In another section you then advertise "Widgets - Wanted to Buy". You gather widget buyers from one ad, then acquire widgets from the other ad, then mark up what you pay for widgets you purchase from sellers, then sell them for a profit to your widget buyers.

I know that seems too clever and too simple to work, but with some guidance or a little extra knowledge that may take a bit of study, you can make this work with real estate. I'll give you a real estate example I know really does work.

Let's say you call home owners who are advertising their homes for sale directly, no broker: "Home for sale, $200,000". For most people, that implies coming up with $200,000 which further implies qualifying and getting a home loan and all the hoops that entails. But you call and ask the seller if he would consider financing the deal, seller financing, with, say $10,000 down and $1,300 a month payments for 5 years. You'd line up being able to buy the $200,000 home for $10,000 down and you propose to give him a note and mortgage for the remainder of $ 190,000. After talking to a dozen home owners who say no to the idea, one finally says "yes". So, you now have a widget; it's a desirable home on attractive terms and, mainly, no banks to deal with due to the "seller financing".

Next, you advertise "No Bank Qualifying Home" and then ask callers how much they can put down on a home. In time, or if you did this in advance and accumulated several buyers with cash to put down, you look for the one who can put down, say $ 15,000 and is ok with $1,300 a month for 5 years and likes the home.

You have created a very special "widget" to sell by negotiating a deal for a home that the homeowner did not initially offer; attractive, no bank qualifying terms and now you have a widget buyer too.

Now, you can do one of two things. You could buy the home from the seller for $10,000 down and, on the same day, sell it to the end user for $15,000 down, using this end users money to close your deal and you make $5,000 profit. Alternatively, you could sandwich yourself in between the parties if there is a big gap in the price you buy it for and what you sell it for. Say, buy it for $ 200,000 and resell it for $225,000 using the same terms and still getting the $5,000 extra up front and the remaining $20,000 when the end buyer refinanced to pay you off.

If you did not set up an attractive spread, you could just assign the situation as noted and sell your purchase contract to the end user for $ 5,000 and walk away.

Now, you're probably asking what you tell the seller and the end buyer and how do I put this deal together and what documents do I need, etc. Getting into the weeds is not my goal here, but, you get the point, I hope: widgets for sale.

Diversify

I'm all for diversification. If you're a stock and bond person, great. If you're passively invested, letting a name brand brokerage handle your investments, read this book.

It's titled <u>Money – Master the Game</u>, by Tony Robbins. Tony spent five years travelling and talking in person to the top investors in the world. He got them to divulge what they really do, really think, and rarely, if ever, have told anyone. One of the shockers you'll learn about in the book is that many of the big name brokerage have some clever language in their agreements their customers sign than can, over time, consume 40% of more of your profits! And they put that money into their pockets, not yours. Read the book. By the way, Warren Buffet has instructed his wife to invest in <u>*indexed funds*</u>; for your consideration.

The challenge with this type of investing, however, is that you have no control. The headline below suggests Buffett has a good idea. Let's turn to the subject at hand.

 MARKETS   POLITICS   FEATURES   FBN TV

Study Finds 90% Active Funds Not Beating S&P

Cantor Fitzgerald CEO Shawn Matthews discusses a study that shows nine out of 10 equity funds are not beating the market.

Should you consider diversification into real estate or expansion of your current holdings? Specifically, should you consider true income property real estate vs houses? You should, absolutely. It's easier than most think.

About Residential Investing
Most Get This Wrong

The typical starting point for most real estate investors is to buy a home for investment. Most have the idea of buying a home, renting it out, then waiting for inflation to increase the value. Leveraging the deal, by getting a bank loan, minimizes the amount one invests and further boosts the expected return on the investment.

Alternatively, they look for a fixer upper home, hoping to match the impressive results of the rehabbers we see on TV. Let me go into a little depth on each of these ideas, then I'll show you some other, more clever ways to make money with homes. Here are the pros and cons of these approaches.

Inflation Investing

Let's assume you buy a $200,000 home in good condition and a good location and put down 20% which would be $40,000. You get a bank loan for the balance of $160,000. You then rent it out with a goal of selling it a few years down the road for let's say, $225,000.

In a perfect world, if you sold that home, say 3 years later, and the mortgage paid down by $6,000 due to amortization, you'd sell for $225,000 and pay off the mortgage balance of $154,000 for a gross profit of $71,000 ($225,000 - $154,000 = $71,000). After deducting the original investment of $40,000 that leaves a profit on $31,000. Over 3 years, that's an average annual return of 25.83 % per annum. That's an excellent return, but, of course, I've left out some important details.

After you buy, you may have a few months in carrying costs before you get a renter including advertising, mortgage payments and utilities. You may have fix up costs while a tenant is in occupancy. When you go to sell the home, you'll need to get rid of the renter before you clean up the place to put it on the market. It's next to impossible to sell an occupied home. If the tenant had to move out during your holding period, you'd have clean up and fix up costs, carrying costs of your mortgage payment with no rent to offset it.

When you sell it, you may need a Realtor and that can run 5% to 7% of your end sales price, plus you'll pay closing costs of about another 2% of your sales price. You get the picture. The $31,000 hoped-for profit can be eaten up fast and that 25.83% return begins to vanish. This is a losing proposition and most people who try this find themselves getting out of the real estate investing business.

Fixer Homes

We see this method of investing on TV: the home rehab shows. The profits can be very tempting. Here's how this works in reality. Let's say you buy a home with a $200,000 target value, usually known as "after repair value" (ARV). That's the value that similar homes in the area, in good condition, have sold for. Let's say the estimated fix up costs, carrying costs, loan costs and end marketing costs total $30,000.

To make a profit, you need to buy that home for about 60% to 70% of the ARV <u>less</u> the fix up costs. So, 65% of the ARV of $200,000 = $130,000 <u>less</u> $30,000 in costs = $100,000 target purchase price. If all goes well, you can make a profit of $70,000 ($200,000 less $100,000 purchase less $30,000 in costs).

What you don't see is this. These TV investor make lots of offers. I mean a lot. They may make 15 to 30 offers or more to find one deal that fits this financial mold. Many have a system to find deals, make offers, negotiate, inspect, estimate costs, and market the homes they buy. It's a business, not a hobby or sideline. In addition, they face a lot of competition from other investors doing the same thing. You see the easy part on TV; the part after the real work has been done. In short, these investors have made their money when they did all the pre-purchase steps right. The "fix up" is just the mechanics to extract their profit in the end. As you see during this part, costs can and usually do exceed expectations, but that's where the 60% to 70% factor comes into play; lots of leeway for surprises. One trick. If you can contract to buy a fixer near the fomula noted, you can sell that contract to a fixer investor. You usually get paid when he closes. $5,000 to $10,000 is not an unusual fee to receive. This is called "wholesaling". You make a profit and never swing a hammer. You can "wholesale" most any good deal, residential or commercial.

These two ideas, buy-rent-sell and fixer homes, are what most people understand as the main opportunities to "get into real estate". There are smarter ways to approach single family homes for less money, less risk, and still make an excellent profit. They are noted below. I'll then show you how to do the same thing with commercial and apartment properties with more profit potential, far less competition, and a road map to create life time cash flow without more work.

The Big Pay Off From Seller Financing

Before we continue, here's something to understand. Knowing this can have a positive impact on your pocket book regardless of whether you're a seller or a buyer. Real estate involves two major components, debt and equity. Here's a simple primer on how an existing mortgage can work to your advantage if you're a seller or if you wish to convince a seller from whom you are buying to carry back a mortgage so you won't have to get a new loan and deal with a lender (you want to avoid that). This works the same with commercial properties, but I'll use a house to make the point.

The market value of your home is $200,000 but you can get more for it when the buyer does not have to go through the hoops to get a new loan. If you sold it traditionally for cash and paid a Realtor and some closing costs, you'd pay out about $16,000 on a $200,000 sale. With a $175,000 underlying loan balance, you'd walk away with $9,000 from the traditional sale. Remember that number: $9,000. Alternatively, let's assume you offer to sell the home via "seller financing, no bank qualifying" and you sell it for $212,000. You ask for $12,000 down. The deal is fast and easy. You pay some closing costs of, say, $2,000 for title insurance, closing fees, etc and walk away with $10,000 in your pocket plus…something very interesting financially remains for you:

They now owe you $200,000 which you carry back in a note and mortgage. You are "the bank" and they make monthly payments to you, let's say at interest only at 7% per annum, or $1,166 per month and they agree to refinance and pay you off in 5 years. Let's say your current loan payments are $1,077 per month, so you keep $89 a month from the differential. Their $200,000 obligation to you is "wrapped around" your current mortgage on which you owe the $175,000 at the time of sale. Over the next 5 years, their balance owed to you does not change as they are paying you interest only. Even if you did amortize their loan, this still works great. However, your balance owed goes down every month on your existing mortgage, thereby increasing your equity at pay off.

5 years later when they pay you off with a new loan, depending on your original loan amortization, you may only owe say $154,000. There are no Realtor commissions or other fees when they pay you off. You now walk away with $46,000 at the closing of their refinance! That's in addition to the $10,000 you kept up front on the seller financed sale, and the $89 a month differential you got for 5 years which is an additional $5,340.

Summed up, if you were to have originally sold for cash using a Realtor, after costs, you'd have walked away with $9,000. With this seller financed approach, you will earn $61,340 ! Worth knowing.

Low Risk Ways to Make Money with Homes & Commercial Properties

Here are some low risk ways to make money with homes that will be a foundation for our commercial income property investing coming up.

        Options
        Lease Options
        Wholesaling
        Seller Financing
        Getting the Deed
        Retailing

OPTIONS

An "option" is a written agreement between you and an owner giving you the right to perform an agreed type of transaction, or several types, with the prices & terms outlined in the agreement. Usually, this is for a set period of time. A "option fee" may or may not be included, and that fee may be as little as $10.

The best deal structures (Widgets) to seek from a home seller are these.

        Lease Option

        Seller Financed Sale

        Buy for Cash at a Discount

Here are the two key types of options:

Open Option

In this method, the seller has no obligation to you if he makes other arrangements before you perform. They are easy to arrange. Option fees are not set. In fact, there is no standard option fee to relate to. A $10 option fee is certainly possible.

Exclusive Option

In this arrangement, any deal of his or yours goes through you. You have full control of the property. Again, option fees are not set. The difference in the open and exclusive option is set up in the agreement you both sign. Personally, I usually choose the Open Option, because few people object to it and I can usually out market most owners.

When This Works

Remember, this works best when the owner is offering a home for sale, with the expectation of an all cash sale in which his buyer must get a new loan. Alternatively, they may be offering the home "for rent". What you are doing is creating attractive terms for a niche market of special buyers the owner has not considered. Examples will follow.

How You Make Money

The first of the two ways your make money with these methods is to sandwich yourself in between the owner and the tenant-buyer or buyer if the spread or mark up between the price and terms you work out with the owner as compared with what you arranged with the tenant – buyer. By the way, I'll refer to "tenant-buyers", meaning it could be a tenant with a lease & option to buy or a buyer who has purchased with seller financing.

If the spread is small, and you'll see examples upcoming, you may want to "assign" the deal you've worked out with the owner directly to the tenant-buyer for a fee, paid by the buyer.

LEASE OPTIONS

Here is a typical situation from my experience of the situation I found to most easily make this idea work. You offer to lease the home from the owner at a fixed end price and terms (number of years and rent rate) with the <u>right to sublease</u> the home to a tenant buyer or <u>to assign</u> the deal with these attractive terms to a tenant buyer.

Home Value: Comps Range from $210 to $235 K

Owner owes $ 195,000 (this small spread between value and amount owed is why he's not using an agent. He may be offering the home for rent as well.

Owner Moved – Vacant / Owner has two homes and two payments

Main Concern $ 1,250 mo extra payment

Plan: Offer to lease option the home from owner for $215,000 option price with $1,000 (or less) option fee down. Again, there is no expected or "normal" option fee. It's non-refundable to you. Alternatively you may offer no option fee, just a rental deposit, say $1,000 which is refundable or credited toward the purchase price, as either would be. I would usually get a one year lease with the right to extend for two additional one year periods. This way, my only exposure is a one year lease, not longer, unless I wish to exercise the extension periods. Also, if you can negotiate a later start date, that is the payment would begin 60 or 90 days after signing the agreement, do so. You could add in that that payments would start when you got a tenant buyer in the home too, but "not more than 90 days out". This may be easier to get the owner to agree to.

I'd include in my proposal the right to sublet to tenant buyer and look to make my lease payment of, say, $1,250 equal to his payment.

You offer to pay first $250 of any single instance repairs after the first 30 days of occupancy. You'll require the same of the tenant buyer so no cost to you.

If you wish, you can assign the lease option you've worked out with the owner to a buyer, charging the buyer a fee and executing the paperwork.

What's in it For The Owner – Seller ?

- Pay Down of Mortgage – the typical $ 250,000 Mortgage a few year old may pay down an average of $375 / mo. Over 5 years, that's $22,500 benefit the owner receives when paid off due to the loan reduction being paid by you and you're paid by the tenant buyer.
- If you act as investor, no Realtor cost to seller. This saves $ 15,000 or more.

You've given the owners a choice of getting $37,500 more to work with you ($22,500 in amortization pay down + $15,000 Realtor fee saved) versus his alternative of a possible break even sale if done the normal way with an agent or even lose money on a sale. Of most interest to the seller, at first, is relief from current payments, his main motivation.

How to Profit With What You've Set Up

Secure a lease-option tenant buyer for a $ 235,000 end price. Arrange lease payments of, say $1,475 / mo. Require an option fee, non-refundable, from them to you of $5,000 or more. It's a good idea not to advertise the option fee you want, just ask what they have to work with. You may get more than you expected. This is credited toward the end price if they buy, so the balance due you at end sale from them is $230,000. The seller is due $214,000 per your lease option with owner after getting credit for the $1,000 option fee you paid them, if you did it this way.

Upon the tenant buyer getting a new loan and cashing this deal out, you net $16,000 plus $4,000 net from option fees. That's a $ 20,000 profit plus the monthly cash flow from differential of rents. I'd typically give the tenant buyer a one year lease with the right to extend for second year. If they moved out, say during the first year, offer it again to another tenant buyer and pick up another $5,000 or more.

What if you could not arrange a decent profit spread like this ? Let's say the market value range was slim. If you could offer the same terms and price as you'd worked out with the seller and only marked up the option fee due from the tenant buyer to $ 5,000 (tenant buyer pays you $ 6,000 and you pay the seller $1,000) you could assign this deal to the tenant buyer for this upcharge and walk away with $ 5,000.

So, whether you select a sandwich position or an assignment, done right, this is creating money from nothing.

Lease Option or Lease Purchase? These terms are often used interchangeably. A lease option gives you the right but not the obligation to buy. A lease purchase creates an obligation to buy. However, the option fee (or "purchase fee" as it's called in the case of a lease-purchase) may be the same in both situations and the only loss, the only recourse by the owner, to you if you do not perform.

I prefer lease options as there is less confusing "expectation" as a "lease purchase" may imply. I also create a lease option for the tenant buyer too. One other feature to the tenant buyer is that while they have an option to buy from you for a fixed price, they also then have the right to sell for a profit if they can get more than their option price. Or at least, they may get back their option fee if they secure and end buyer or a new tenant buyer to take their place.

Finally, always get, in advance, a title report and the loan balance(s) information (the "note") on the mortgage(s) of homes you get involved with. You don't want to get a surprise down the road of tax liens or a mortgage greater than your option price with the owner. Some old forms or mortgage also had an accrual feature that increased the mortgage balance over time in exchange for the homeowners getting lower payments.

Of course, always get and attorney to review your documents and disclosures you plan to use with all parties. It's a very good idea to pay an attorney to close the deal with both the parties in his office too. This will add to the comfort of all parties.

Always check with a title company (or attorney if it's common in your state to use them vs title companies) and a mortgage lender before you move forward to determine how you can collect on this kind of deal when the tenant buyer closes. You may need proof of a publically recorded option, though you should always get that. The title report the tenant buyers lender receives will not show you as the owner, so you'll want to create the right paper trail to resolve this. I'd recommend that all payments to you from the tenant buyer (you pay the owner with these funds if it's a sandwich deal) go through an escrow company so you'll have third party proof of a good payment history when the tenant buyer applies for a loan.

In the following chart, I've shown the details and key profit centers of a lease option deal which include __option fee spread__, __price spread__, __rental spread__, and other items, like a price credit from the seller for each lease payment made, that will boost returns which include negotiating a credit for yourself with the owner for each rent payment which goes to reduce what you own the seller when you close. It all adds up. An **852% return** is shown here over an appx 2 year investment term. After you get back you investment with the tenant buyers' option fee, you have no investment left in the deal, early on. With tenant buyers lined up or a cheap option, you can reduce your initial outlay to near zero.

Single Home LEASE OPTION Cash Flow Highlights

TB- Tenant Buyer who occupies and eventually owns the home
HO- Home Owner from whom you lease option the home

Option Price to Tenant Buyer	$215,000		
Your Option Price with Owner	$190,000		
Locked in Potential Profit	$25,000		

Acquisition & Start Up Costs

	$1,500	to HO	Option Fee ($1000) and Rent Deposit ($500)
	$0		1st Months Rent - Negotiate first 30 days free-HO got fee & dep
	$1,175		Month 2 Rent
	$175		Interim Utlities
	$200		Signs / Lock box / some marketing
	$3,050		total acquistion cost
	$5,000		TB Option Deposit
Net Cost	**$1,950**	Positive	Net Cost after Receipt of Tenant Buyers Option Deposit is a positve cash flow. No money left in the deal.

Carry Period Profit

Your Rent to Owner	$ 1,175 / Mo	
Your Rent from TB	$ 1,350 / mo	
Net Cash Flow	$ 175 / mo	Assume TB buys in 18 months
18 months x $ 175	**$3,150**	Carry cost Profit
		TB pays first $ 250 of any repair
		landlord (HO) pays any in excess

Net Profit before end sale   **$5,100**   Net Income to Date
    Virtually no investment outstanding
    but this much ahead

End Sale Profit

		$20,000	Option spread due less $ 5,000 credit to TB
	plus	900	$50 per month credit from HO x 18 months
			TB may or may not receive credits during lease period
		$20,900	
	plus	$5,100	Net profit Income prior to end sale
Total Profit		**$26,000**	

Return on original Outlay   **852.00** % $ 26,000 / $ 3050

COMMENTS

1. There is a lot of room for error. We're even offering realtors $ 1500 to promote to owners to whom we make offers.
2. These are nice homes in nice areas, not fix ups. They are in move in condition
3. If a TB does not buy, you clean up the home, get another TB and collect another $ 5,000
4. The $5,000 TB option deposit is not fixed but is typical. $ 3,500 to $ 8,000 has been my experience but $ 5000 has become my minimum except on less expensive homes
5. Home prices are in the area of most desired and highest sales volume neighborhoods. Always FHA qualified.
6. If a home does not work out for any reason, you are only obligated to a lease. Worst case, lease the home to others and abandon the lease at the end of the term. You've not siged a bank loan, just a lease.
7. All maintenace costs and all end sales costs are passed through to tenant buyer.
8. Buy using an Option with the owner to lease option the home, one could by-pass the obligation to take on the cost of leasing the home before you obtained a tenant buyer.

WHOLESALING

Wholesaling is the activity of passing bargains on to bargain hunters. You control the property by a contract rather than through an option or lease option. Here is what you are doing. You are typically finding a rehab home, contracting to buy it, then passing this contract on to a cash, fixer buyer, for a markup over your contracted price.

In the previous rehab example, you may have contracted to buy the $100,000 current value deal for $95,000 then sold your contract for $5,000 to a rehabber. Or, if you contracted to buy it for $100,000 you might be able to mark it up by $5,000. Either way, it's about buying it right so there is a comfortable profit for the rehabber. You are usually paid by the rehabber when he closes the deal.

In the case of homes, you are dealing with lenders who may add stipulations to you as buyer that you close the deal in the buyer name you contracted with. You may need to close with transactional funds (a one day loan) then resell to the rehab buyer or you may set up a "land contract" or LLC and then let the rehab buyer get involved via these vehicles. You should always check with a title company closer to learn what they are seeing going on in the current market. If you are buying a foreclosed, bank owned deal or a short sale (defaulted owner signs your contract but the defaulted lender calls the shots and the price) you'll want to know the current lender requirements and regulations and how these deals are getting done. Regardless, know your exit strategy and always get legal advice from an experienced real estate attorney.

The best way to get involved in a wholesale deal is to work directly with a defaulted owner if possible. Auctions and bank owned deals create challenges to someone wholesaling deals to other parties, but it can be accomplished if you plan ahead.

SELLER FINANCING

Seller financed deals work similar to lease option deals. You buy for one price with a small down payment & mutually agreed terms (monthly payment, length of the term, & price) then secure a buyer for a mark-up on price and the down payment. The main difference, if you stay sandwiched in, is that you have a pay-off obligation that you don't have with a lease option deal. A $200,000 purchase with $15,000 down arrangement with the seller, via an option or contract, is then resold to an end buyer for $230,000 with $25,000 down. You assign your deal to the end buyer for $10,000 profit or stay sandwiched in if the spread is attractive. You still get the $10,000 but there's $20,000 left in this deal for you between what the end buyer owes you after his down payment or $205,000 vs $185,000 due the seller from whom you bought after your down payment to him, using the end buyer's money.

GETTING DEEDS

There are many situations in which an owner will deed you their property in exchange for your taking over the payments. This called taking a property "subject to" meaning you are NOT applying to take over the existing loan, as the loan remains in the owners' name, but you will make the payments as you both agree.

Yes, you are getting a "free house" and can lease it, lease option it out to a tenant buyer, seller finance it to a buyer or sell it for cash if there's enough equity between what you can sell if for and what is owed.

An example; the owner deeds you a property subject to a $190,000 mortgage balance with payments of $ 1,300 a month and you give him $ 2,000 for this deed and you agree you'll pay him off in 5 years so he's out from under the loan. You now make the payments (always to an escrow company so you know the underlying mortgage is being paid, with any excess going to the seller). Now you can lease option or seller finance the property. Say you sell it for $ 210,000 with $ 10,000 down, with the balance due in 3 years. You've made a profit of $8,000 up front (less any mortgage payments and carrying costs after the deed transfer) and have another $10,000 due when your buyer gets a loan to pay you off within 3 years ($ 200,000 due you from end buyer and you owe seller $ 190,000 (or less depending on how you agreed to share the pay down of the mortgage over the term).

The secret to doing this? Just ask if they will sell for what they owe. You can also leave some equity on the table for them, due when you eventually cash out the deal. Providing "moving money" for an owner occupant to move if they have not already done so can be a good incentive.

IN SUMMARY

What you have done with these methods is to control property without ownership in the traditional sense. You've not gotten a bank loan for yourself or put up big money to get this control. Options and contracts are the way to control a property for limited periods. Negotiating lease options or seller financing terms are methods for creating attractive proposals for end buyers which the owner may not have considered nor offered. You then are offering a property with attractive, no bank qualifying terms to a large segment of the market who may not currently qualify for a home loan. You are creating high demand widgets by negotiating terms with owners, then offering them to widget buyers and making a profit. Sometimes, it's money from thin air as you will have put out little if any investment.

SOURCES OF LEADS

In addition to seeking deals from owners offering their homes for sale or for rent directly (no agent), there are lots of ways to secure opportunities. Entire courses have been created for many of these, but a systemized approach to making contact and offers can be done on your own. Here are few others:

Defaulted Loan Lists
Divorce
Job Transfer
Job Loss
Probate Lists
Fire Damage
Out of town owners, to name a few.

THE SECRET TO SUCCESS WITH ALL OF THIS – A MOTIVATED SELLER!

If there is one underlying key to all these deals I've outlined and the commercial opportunities I'll be showing you, it's to find a motivated seller. You do not talk anyone into these opportunities for yourself. You are looking for owners who just want out ! Now, every imaginable situation can create these situations; divorce, deaths, business or personal financial difficulty, legal battles, and more. Your goal is just to find them and offer solutions from which you can benefit and they can be relieved of a perceived burden.

The owner of that first deal I ever did, out with the horses (see the appendix), called me years later for advice on what to do about a real estate matter she needed resolved. I'd solved her problem. One of my favorite lease option deals I did was with an attorney with the US Justice Dept. who had been transferred and did not want to rent out his home in the traditional way. I showed up and the idea that I was an investor who'd be responsible for the home and putting in and helping the tenant buyer made his day. I went through 2 lease option tenants and collected $ 11,500 total in option fees and made a $ 25,000 additional profit on the end sale to a tenant buyer who was a mortgage lender it turns out. This was only an $185,000 home, by the way. So, you are not short changing anyone. You are taking them out of a stressful or unwanted situation. Discard the many who will have other agendas or are not open to your ideas. The motivated ones are the flexible, easy ones to work with.

I did enough lease options, all were sandwich deals, that I wrote my first book with the details of finding them, offering and marketing them, and more. About 95% of this book also applies to seller financed deals, and, with the idea of assignments, you could earn the $2,500 seed capital noted in the title by doing an assignment deal first, then you can move to actually lease a place with a good spread.

THE KEY POINT IS THAT THESE METHODS THAT SAVVY INVESTORS USE FOR RESIDENTIAL DEALS CAN BE APPLIED TO COMMERCIAL PROPERTIES WHERE THERE IS FAR LESS COMPETITION

Control without Ownership and ZERO Down Investing

You can CONTROL properties for short term periods with these methods:

        1. Options
        2. Contracts
        3. Letters of Intent

You can control properties for longer periods by using:

        1. Leases with Options to Buy – Sandwiched in a lease option
        2. Being Sandwiched in a Seller Financed Transaction
        3. Getting Ownership Transferred to You by A Deed

Your profit by
1. Assigning your position (for Quick Seed Capital)

2. Same day sale of a property (for Quick Seed Capital)

3. Getting sandwiched in on a lease option, deed transfer, or seller financed situation and cashing out at the end when an end user concludes a purchase. (medium term Seed Capital)

4. Owning, upgrading and reselling a property.

Returns on investment using these ideas can be in the 100% even 1,000% return on invested capital, even infinite if you consider some situations require no investment. Remember the widget example? Without dissecting each idea here, I'll show you how a few can be used to make money.

<u>In short, homes can be good investments for short term (2 minutes to 2 years) profit, but are poor long term investments as the value of the home vs the net rent they can generate does not work to your advantage.</u> The alternative is to consider true income properties. Here are some real world examples of what one can do with these ideas just noted, for seed capital, a prelude to true income property investing for passive cash flow.

2,800 SF Office Condo - A $25,000 PROFIT – Zero Investment – Zero Risk – Assigned Contract. Set Up with One Letter, A Contract, & One Free Ad on a Commercial Offerings Site Web. Here's another:

A VACANT 4 PLEX
$ 38,000 PROFIT – Zero Investment – Zero Risk – Assigned Contract

From local agent's MLS, a Contract, One Ad on Craig's List. My end buyer paid me $148,000: my contract was for $ 110,000. He'll invest appx $20,000 and have a $250,000 property when upgraded and leased up. Win-Win.

You can make good money with PRETTY HOUSES TOO, not just fixers, without buying or owning them.

Invested $2,000 (a deposit and first month's rent) and got back $ 11,000 in short order (a tenant buyers option fee), then another $ 25,000 on end sale. I never owned it, just leased it with an option to buy. This was a $185,000 home, by the way. That's a net profit of $34,000. Homes aren't good income properties, by the way, but fine for earning seed capital like this. Moderate priced homes, mid-market price range, are best for this.

In summary: three properties earned $25,000 + $38,000 + $ 34,000 = $ 97,000

That's just the seed capital part and you don't need that much to get started as an income property investor. The goal is to buy and own passive income properties.

I'll go into detail about how these two commercial deals were put together shortly.

Investor Turns $1 Into $106,525

One more deal I really appreciate. It was not a deal I did like the preceding ones, but I got the details direct from the investor who did it. A bank owned a 3,800 SF foreclosed, vacant building & wanted $100,000 for it. The investor arranged to pay the bank $1 for an option to buy it for $78,000 cash and the right to advertise it. The investor then offers it for sale for $150,000 with <u>Zero Down,</u> and seller financing for 30 years note at a 10.5% rate, due in 10 years with the requirement the buyer pays for the fix up, about $20,000. A buyer is secured quickly. Lots of business owners would jump at the opportunity to own a building and use their money to pay solely for their tenant improvements. The investor then goes to another bank for a $78,000 loan to pay off the owning bank. Bank 2 want 15% down ($11,700) and there are $2,000 in closing costs, so the investor needs $13,700 to close the loan with bank 2 and pay off bank 1 and complete his seller financed sale to the end user. He offers 33% of the deal to another investor who puts up the $13,700. Result?
The investor is out zero, well the $1, and as the new bank loan pays off over7 years he collects the income from the buyers note to cover the bank loan payments. With the net payments received over the 10 year term plus the final balance at payoff he'll receive $159,787 net of all costs: 1/3 goes of this goes the investor who put up the $13,700 and for the <u>$1, this investor keeps $106,525</u>. That's what I refer to as Cash Cow investing! The point is that having an understanding of value, particularly the projected value of a property, one can do some amazing things. So, how do you value an income property? I'll show you the formula shortly.

These are merely to illustrate that when you have a motivated seller, many opportunities open up to you if you understand how to estimate maximum value, current status and the approximate cost to get from one to the other. It's quite easy with commercial income properties as I'll show you. But discard the idea that you have to come up with money to make money. You do not. Knowledge and action alone can be very profitable. These zero down ideas are a way to earn seed capital if that is your desire or need. If you have money to start with, and knowledge, you can accelerate the process.

Investing In & Profiting From Small Apartment & Commercial Properties

I've noted below some of the key reasons to become a true income property investor. Besides the huge demand & high competition for residential fixer deals one ultimately had to deal with end buyers who must qualify for a loan, if don't wholesale them. That's it's own long process. These loans are getting more difficult to complete as government regulations make the process long and complex for home buyers. Just for clarification, let me note that I call all commercial and apartment properties "income" properties: apartments, office buildings, shopping centers, warehouse-industrial, lodging properties and hybrids.

Why Invest In Small Commercial Properties?

- Greater array of opportunities
- Larger profit potential
- Cash buyers are not unusual & financing is much easier than with homes
- Simple to evaluate
- Few people understand small commercial deals so you can fish in big pond with few other fishermen
- You can build a high cash flow portfolio repeating a simple process.
  This allows an "end" goal of <u>*ongoing cash flow and no more deal making*</u>

You can deal at any level you wish, but I suggest you stay with $ 100,000 to $ 1 million deals (possibly up to $ 3 million). Professional investors don't have time to do "small deals" like these leaving the field wide open for you. Your location may adjust these dollar amounts a bit, but as a broad suggestion, apartments under 50 units and commercial deals under 25,000 square feet are good targets. You can make money with duplexes and triplexes, but I don't consider these good multi-family properties. The smallest to consider are 4-plexes an up. Direct contact with owners versus agents, in my experience, will allow you do this more easily and without much, if any, competition.

Moving from home investment and taking some of these ideas forward that I've mentioned, one can make even more money with small commercial income properties. There is little competition and few people, including many who own these properties, understand establishing value or value creation.

This means a huge, nationwide opportunity for you. Here are the foundation principles:

-- Homes are Valued on Comparable, Area Home Sales
-- Commercial Properties are Valued on Comparable Capitalization Rates (Cap Rates)
-- Cap Rates are applied to Well Occupied Properties – Good Condition

For properties in trouble or not operating as they could, the cap rate concept falls apart. I'll show you how this applies in just a moment. This confusion creates a potential gold mine for profit if you know a few basics. These two concepts apply:

MARKET RENTS LIMIT VALUE

CAPITALIZATION ESTABLISHES VALUE

This applies to ALL COMMERCIAL PROPERTIES:

- **Apartments**

- **Office Buildings (*single or multi-tenant)**

- **Shopping Centers (*single or multi-tenant)**

- **Warehouses and their hybrids (*single or multi-tenant)**

- **Hotel and Motels - these are businesses wrapped in real estate but the same method of valuation applies. I don't agree with this, but it's a fact.**

* Single tenant properties, and often multitenant ones, are sometimes set up on a *net leased* basis in which the tenant pays some or all of the expenses of the property. As owner, you get a monthly rent check with little or zero upkeep or costs.

What's Truly Possible & the Key To Lifetime, Passive Cash Flow

I'm about to save you 40 years of experimentation. Actually, I'll save you over one thousand years of throwing darts in the dark, financially, in real estate investing if you consider what's been learned during the years of experience of all my clients, collectively. I've been able to look over the shoulders of a lot of investors, many of whom were among the best at what they do. Here's the pay off.

If you include the very clever ideas, many learned from savvy residential investors, noted in the preceding Control Without Ownership list, it all comes together in what I branded as the Cash Cow Investing Plan. It is this:

> **Earn Seed Capital**
> **Invest in a First Income Property**
> **Parlay that One Into Many for Passive, Lifetime Cash Flow**

If you already have seed capital, you can save yourself about one year of effort. Starting with appx $50,000 to $100,000 and buying properties at appx 75% of after repair value (that includes purchase price, financing and fix up costs) you can extract most or all your invested capital upon refinance and KEEP the property you invested in and the cash flow if generates. And with your refunded capital, you can do it again…. and again.

<u>In short, one could, in principle, go from zero to a first investment to parlaying that one into many so that at the end of appx 5 years you could have passive income of appx. $85,000 a year, a net worth of appx $ 1,100,000 and cash in the bank, from the last refinance, of appx $350,000.</u>

Now, this is an extreme end, buying distressed properties, of how one can profit from income properties. There are a lot of options in between. This is detailed more in my <u>Cash Cows</u> book but there are other profit ranges noted in the General Income Property Opportunities chart noted later in this report.

Not everyone has the temperament to take on this extreme profit types of projects, but the risks can be greatly minimized. If someone is happy with a more hassle free income property investment and annual returns in the 9% to 15% range, that's easier to do & more plentiful. I work with clients on both ends of the spectrum and in between. Further on, I'll show you this wide array of opportunities to profit with income properties, from income increases to operational efficiencies to how all these financial improvements are then greatly multiplied by capitalization. Let's look at that next.

Homes Vs Income Properties

Houses are bought and sold within their market place based on what others are paying for similar homes. You can't sell a home for $325,000 in a neighborhood in which there are multiple sales in the $190,000 to $ 225,000 range. It doesn't matter if you gold plate the fixtures, tile the garage floor, paint the driveway with silver leaf, and put a waterfall that cascades into an Olympic-sized pool in the back yard. You might get a few bucks more with these features, but not much. You certainly won't get back your investment or even close. More important, if you rent out your house, say for $1400 a month or even $2,000 a month, that income will not increase the value. People don't buy homes for income, or shouldn't. Income does not define home values. Only what people pay for homes they plan to live in define residential values.

Only true income properties are bought, sold and valued based on their income. True income properties include office buildings, shopping centers, apartments, warehouses, and lodging properties. One of the things I noticed early in my income property brokerage career was that the smart investors, and not all are smart, were not interested in seeing the property as a first step. That came later. What they wanted first were the P&L's (profit and loss) statements for a couple or three years back. You'll see why further on. The first thing a home buyer wants to do is see the house. So, what's going on?

The Magic Formula for All Income Property Types

Here's the formula upon which all income property values revolve. With this, and a bit of knowledge about how to fill in the figures, a whole world of profitable opportunities unfolds.

Annual Income

minus   (Annual Expense)

Net Operating Income

minus   (Debt Service)   (mortgage payments)

Cash Flow

Gross Potential Income	$1,000,000
Less: Vacancy & Collection Loss	(60,000)
Effective Gross Income (actual)	940,000
Less: Expenses	(600,000)
Net Operating Income (NOI)	340,000 ⬅
Less: Debt Service	(261,800)
Cash Flow	$ 78,200

Then NOI / CAPTIALIZATION RATE = THE PROPERTY VALUE

$ 340,000 / .08 (8% Cap Rate) = $ 4,250,000
$ 340,000 / .07 (7% Cap Rate) = $ 4,857,142
$ 340,000 / .09 (9% Cap Rate) = $ 3,777,777

<u>The capitization rate defines the annual return on investment for an all cash purchase: using the 7% cap rate sample above, you write a check for $4,857,142 and you get a 7% ($340,000), the NOI, return in year one.</u>

<u>This is the key formula for all income property types</u> and how value is determined based on the income; specifically, the net operating income or NOI. This concept works for well

rented properties in good condition. If work needs to be done today to maintain this income, that cost would be subtracted from the determined value.

Now, a funny thing happens when a property is underperforming or has lower occupancy than it should, like an apartment at 80% occupancy vs 92% occupancy or with rents well below market. The magic formula for determining value gets muddled and is of little use.

Let's use the example above. Let's assume the occupancy is 80% and the expenses are the same as shown (they don't drop much with a drop in occupancy). That lowers the effective gross income to $ 800,000 and the net income, thereby, to $200,000. If one capitalizes this $ 200,000 NOI at an aggressive 7%, that suggests a value of $2,857,142. That's a difference of $ 1,999,992 from the 7% cap value at 94% occupancy.

What happens in real life is that the seller is not usually going to stand for such a low price. In fact, he may owe more than this and unless he agrees to enter into a short sale, in which the sale would be for less than the current mortgage balance and the seller gets nothing, all that's left is negotiating between the buyer, that's you, and the seller who owns this troubled property.

Let's say he wants to get $3,600,000. The capitalization rate applied to the current $200,000 NOI would need to be 5.5% to create this value. If you were looking for a good deal and saw an apartment for sale at 5.5% cap rate when most were selling for 7% cap rates, you'd miss an opportunity if you did not look further at this anomaly to learn it was a good upside possibility. Again, a negotiation is in order. Knowing how to calculate the end or target value, less a few cost-to-get there figures, can produce a big profit. More is covered in my <u>Cash Cows</u> book and home study course, but this is how opportunities exist in the real world.

A final digression to simplify capitalization. You are negotiating, whether a buyer or seller, around a specific number, the NOI, when you capitalize it. If I'm selling, getting a buyer to accept a low rate of return, like 7%, means I can sell at a higher price. If my buyer wants an 8% return, not the 7% I'm offering, he'll pay less for this NOI. Hope that helps. See the 7-8-9% cap rates and the related values on the chart again with this in mind. I've dealt with millionaire commercial real estate developers who still don't get this, so we'll go a little deeper. Most small income property owners have no understanding of this either. Buried in the many income property offerings that are often grossly overpriced, by a seller who likely overpaid in the first place, you can find some gems that can create a very big payday for those willing to learn what I'm showing you here.

As one of my mentors is fond of saying, Dan Kennedy, marketing guru of guru's: *"Most people fail in life and business because they are looking for simple solutions to complex problems." Amen, Dan!*

Capitalization Multiplies Your Efforts

$ 100 a month in increased revenue or decreased expense:

$ 1,200 per year to the NOI (net operating income)

Capitalized at 8.5 %

WORTH $ 14,117 in new VALUE

$ 100 mo -> $ 14,117

Only with commercial properties

ASSUMES GOOD REPAIR GOOD OCCUPANCY

NOI (annual) / CAP RATE(%) = VALUE

A cap rate is merely the <u>Annual Return</u> a given net operation income will yield on a dspecific price. A 7% annual return is less attractive to a buyer than an 8% return. The buyer is paying for the same NOI. The more he pays, the less his return as we assume, for current value purposes, that the NOI is a fixed figure. The seller gets more by selling a 7% return than an 8% return because the price is higher. As you can see by the chart, the starting point for this determination is the annual rent. For the troubled or poorly operating property, determining the possible or target value of the property only requires a knowledge of market rents and likely expenses you can learn from similar properties, coupled with a cap rate. The cap rates are a function of the market as are rents.

You can find cap rate ranges for each property type in a given area by looking at offerings at www.LoopNet.com: a public MLS for commercial deals. Remember, asking prices are not selling prices, but it will give you an indication of cap rate ranges. They do change over time based on mortgage interest rates but, historically, the lag time is about 2 years. Most investors do not pay all cash. They finance must of the purchase price. That's called leverage and here's how that works:

Leverage

Most investors finance their purchases which creates leverage to minimize their investment and boost their return. Using the example above we have a net operation income of $340,000 per year. Let's assume the median cap rate of 8% to create the purchase price. If we paid all cash for this property and its' $ 340,000 NOI, we'd pay $ 4,250,000. The $340,000 NOI would give us a first year return of 8%. In order to increase that return, most investor, would finance appx 75% of that $ 4,250,000. This would then require a down payment of $1,062,500 (25%) and the new loan would be $3,187,500 (75%). Let's say our loan annual loan cost (debt service) is $223,125 per year (principle and interest). This leaves annual cash flow after the mortgage payments of $116,875. This is an annual return on our 25% ($1,062,500) down payment of 11%, year one if it's stabile over the prior periods you examined. Again, the NOI has not changed. Getting annual loan costs (the percent the total annual payments are to the loan amount) below the cap rate percent will create cash flow above the cap rate on a leveraged purchase.

Perceived Value

In the example above, I've noted 3 cap rates. The 7% cap rate applied to the NOI creates a much greater value than the 9% cap rate as you are getting a buyer to accept a lower rate of return. In fact, it's a very large difference. Even a half percent decrease in cap rate can significantly increase the value of property with no change in NOI. So, the more one can improve a property, the more perceived value it may have. We now get in to perception. If you are buying a car and looking at two and one is dirty and the other is clean, but the cars are identical in every other way, most of us would pay more for the clean car due to a psychologically perceived greater value. This is coupled with a suspicion that the dirty car may have other issues as well. If someone would let a car get so dirty, what else have they let go? So long as an appraiser can find even a modest range of area sales cap rates on similar properties, one can improve a property's look such that an appraiser may lean toward the lower cap rate range and, thereby, a higher value.

As a more graphic example, pop artist Andy Warhol, when his art began to catch on and his prices soared, was asked how he could get such crazy prices for paintings of soup cans and the like. His honest answer was, " I charge whatever I can get away with." Within a reasonable range of rates, cap rates can work like that too.

Is there a "correct" Cap Rate ?
A.W. – "Whatever You Can Get Away With !"

What Andy Warhol said about his art prices applies to both cap rates and rents. The area market will dictate what one can obtain for rents as competition comes into play. Rents, therefore, limit value in a similar way that cap rates do. But neither are set in stone and usually exist within a narrow range in any given market and at any given time. Perception can serve, to some degree, to get a lower cap rate and, thereby, a higher value

Expenses

After the income side of the equation, and I'll get to that, the remaining part of our equations is expenses. In the following chart, I've noted a typical P&L statement showing two prior years then a projected year 1 you might expect after you buy. The next chart is a general P&L showing each property type. The ranges noted in some of them are the result of how an owner may or may not require a tenant to share in annual expenses. This can be the result of what's customary in a given market.

A clearer view of expenses can be gained by looking at offerings of similar property types in a given market. Always get 2 to 3 years of income and expense information about a property under consideration. The operating style of owners comes into play here too. These general ranges are useful in doing initial evaluations to estimate current and target values.

Some comments on the following chart. The more prior years, the better. First, owners of smaller income properties present information in formats that are not uniform. Sometimes, agents will give you limited data, like utilities and taxes only. Don't accept this. You need the real thing or have knowledge about real costs from similar properties.

The reason you want 2 or 3 full years is to separate the wheat from the chaff. Here's what I mean. When an owner compiles his income and expenses, he will likely have his own line item categories. That's fine. Some will be very detailed like "locks, keys, driveway repair, light bulbs, plumbing repairs", etc. More often though, they will be more general like a "maintenance and repairs" line item with a big lump sum figure. Many owners try to max out expenses for tax purposes by including, right or wrong, some personal expenses. That might even include a car purchase. What you are looking for in the expenses is anomalies, from one year to the next. That's why 3 years of expense is better than 2. It's from this information that differences from one year to the next will jump out as you compare them side by side. You can then inquire as to what it was about. If the seller was getting a divorce and lumped in some "legal" expenses into his strip center expenses, you need to know that. Once the anomalies are either removed or modified to fit what you expect personally, you create what I call a "Stabilized" picture of what you're buying. Always remove depreciation and mortgage costs out of expense to calculate net operating income. Depreciation is strictly for tax purposes and mortgage costs goes below the net income line as noted in the formula. One of my clients, selling a Holiday Inn, had some weird expense category tacked on to the bottom of a very detailed P&L (hotels do have a standard format for income and expense, but not everyone uses them). I asked what it was about and he told me it was his personal ranch expenses. That should come out of the expense list, unless you have a ranch and plan to pad your expenses to fool the IRS (not a good idea). As a final check, you'll note at the bottom of the expense column I've calculated the expenses as a percent of income. Assuming a well operating property, with 90% or above occupancy (65% or so for hotels) the percentages I've noted in the <u>General Expense by Property Type</u> chart, are what you should expect. If someone suggests in their information that they are operating their apartment with annual expenses at 35% if gross income, and it's decently occupied, it's either grossly under-rented (doubtful) or someone is kidding someone. You just can't run a true income property that cheaply, unless one is failing to pay all the expenses and the bills are stacking up, but that's another story.

So, in the following chart, I've stabilized 2 years of income and expense, including some estimated assumptions of costs not revealed by the seller early on. This is the starting point to determine the *<u>net operating income</u>* which is the Holy Grail of income property analysis.

More is upcoming about how one who understands this can profit, big time.

INCOME PROPERTY P&L CONSOLIDATION SAMPLE

ANNUAL FIGURES

			2015	2016	STABILIZED
	YEAR				Purchase Yr 1
Income					
	rents		81,655	82,402	
	reimbursements		1565	1,230	
	Total Income		83,220	83,632	83,000
Expenses	Taxes	per seller	10200	10506	10821.18
	Insurance	per seller	1800	1854	1909.62
	Trash	per seller	1928	1986	2045
	Electric	per seller	5100	5253	5410.59
	Gas	per seller	1702	1753	1806
	Water	per seller	734	756	779
	Sewer	per seller	2700	2781	2864.43
	Ads	estimate	500	515	530.45
	Acctg	estimate	500	515	530.45
	Legal	estimate	1200	1236	1273.08
	Snow	estimate	500	515	530.45
	Repairs	estimate	1200	1236	1273.08
	Signage	estimate	1500	1545	1591.35
	Plumbing	estimate	1200	1236	1273.08
	Carpets+	estimate	1500	1545	1591.35
	Hardware	estimate	500	515	530.45
	HVAC	estimate	500	515	530.45
	Mgt	estimate	1200	1236	1273.08
	Misc	estimate	1500	1545	1591.35
	Total Expense		$ 35,964	$ 37,043	$ 38,154
	exp as percent of Inc		43%	44%	46%
Net Operating Income			$ 47,256	$ 46,589	$ 44,846

This, above, I put together from a property in which the seller's agent only gave me the basics to start. I had to pad it with additional "estimates" in other categories until I got more useful numbers. The percent of expense to income near the bottom sets a good rule of thumb method for annual expenses to get to the net operating income, at least initially. I did this, in part, to see if they were covering their debt service. The stabilized column is the starting point to then do a projection, which is upcoming.

WOOKBOOK - PROPERTY EXPENSE CHART

GENERAL EXPENSE PERCENT BY PROPERTY TYPE

As A Percent of Gross Revenue - 90% Occupied
Hotels-Motels 65% Occupied Average

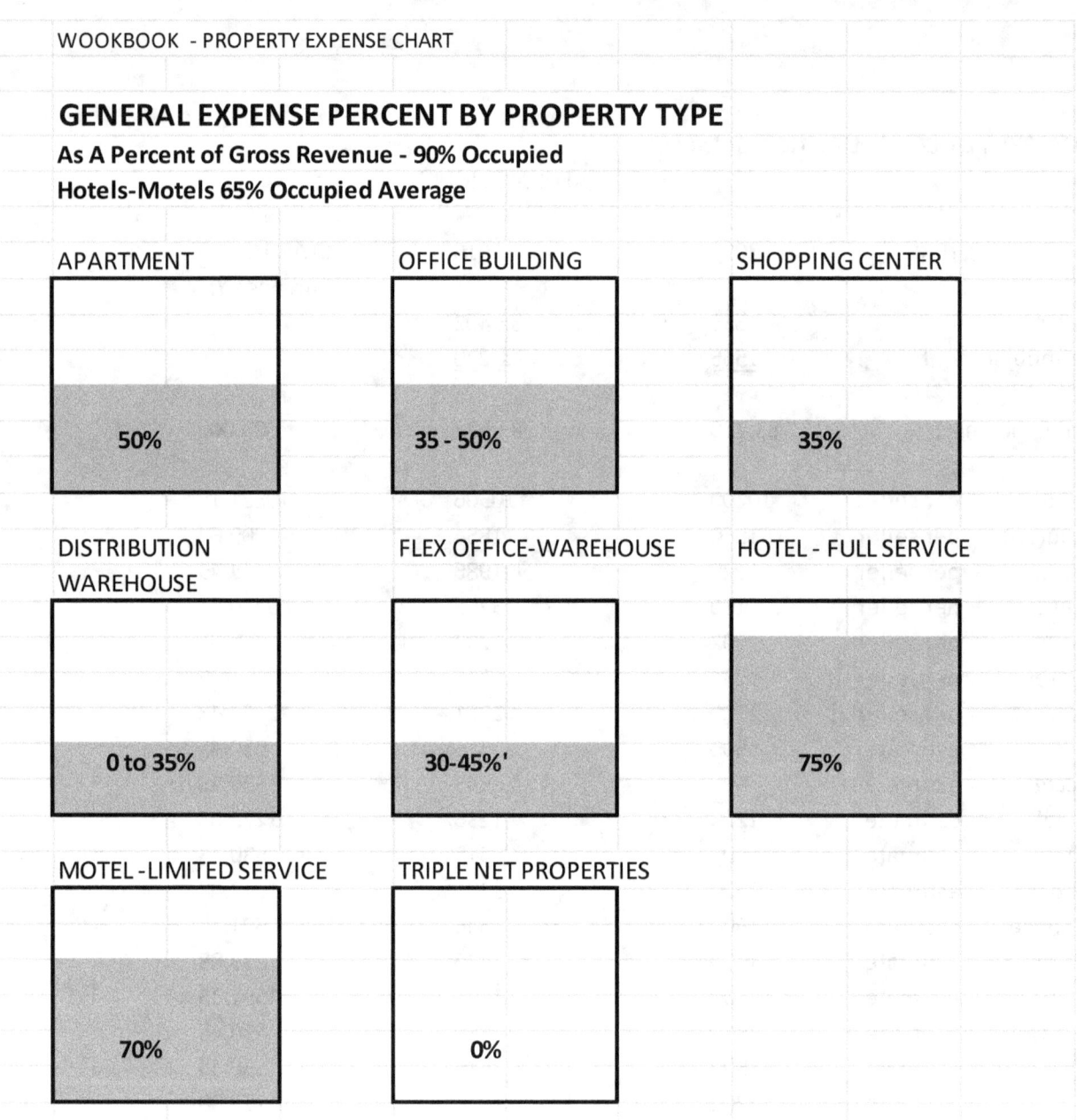

Getting 3 years of annual P&L's plus the current year to date figures will give you average expenses for a given property as this owner has been running the property, which may be too high of two low. <u>*The reward for knowing how to use the simple formula noted and plugging in the numbers for income, expense, and cap rates is that it gives you the keys to the kingdom in dealing in and profiting from all income property types.*</u>

An Income Property Revelation

Let me tell you about a little understood fact that will simplify your understanding of all income property types. The basic layout for all income properties is the same, across the board. Few people realize this as most have focused only on one property type during their career. Home investors don't know what I'm talking about as only comparable sales of similar homes are used to determine their value. This revelation can change the way you pursue income properties and greatly expand your opportunities. Take a look at the next chart. Don't focus so much on the income or expense line items. Back up and look at the 3 blocks on the left side of the chart. They are <u>income</u>, <u>expense</u>, and <u>net operating income</u>. Does this sound familiar? Review the "capitalization" formula and sample

For different income property types, a few line items of income change, the key expenses are the same for all, and only a few property specific expense categories show up.

<u>But the key principle is that the format in which to establish value is the same for all income property types. This understanding allows you to invest in diverse types of income properties.</u>

General Comparison of Income Property P&L's

	Apartment	Office Building	Shopping Center	Warehouses	Motel	Hotel
INCOME	Rents	Rents	Base Rents	Income	Rooms	Rooms
	Utility Reibursements	Parking fees	CAM Reibursements	Reimbursements	Laundry	Food & Beverage
	Laundry		Percentage Rent		Vending	Vending
	Vending				Phone & Internet	Laundry
	Other					Phone & Internet
	Gross Income	**Gross Income**	**Gross Income**	**Gross Income**	**Gross Income**	**Gross Income**
EXPENSE	RE Taxes	RE Taxes	RE Taxes	RE Taxes	RE Taxes	RE Taxes
	Property Insurance	Property Insurance	Property Insurance	Property Insurance	Property Insurance	Property Insurance
	Payroll & PR Taxes	Payroll & PR Taxes	Payroll & PR Taxes	Payroll & PR Taxes	Payroll & PR Taxes	Payroll & PR Taxes
	Janitorial	Janitorial	Janitorial	Janitorial	Janitorial	Janitorial
	Trash Service	Trash Service	Trash Service	Trash Service	Trash Service	Trash Service
	Utilities Gas	Utilities Gas	Utilities Gas	Utilities Gas	Utilities Gas	Utilities Gas
	Elec	Elec	Elec	Elec	Elec	Elec
	Water	Water	Water	Water	Water	Water
	Supplies	Supplies	Supplies	Supplies	Supplies	Supplies
	Prof Management	Prof Management	Prof Management	Prof Management	Prof Management	Prof Management
	Phones	Phones	Phones	Phones	Phones	Phones
	Accounting & Legal	Accounting & Legal	Accounting & Legal	Accounting & Legal	Accounting & Legal	Accounting & Legal
	Maint & Repairs	Maint & Repairs	Maint & Repairs	Maint & Repairs	Maint & Repairs	Maint & Repairs
	HVAC	HVAC	HVAC	HVAC	HVAC	HVAC
	Landscape	Landscape	Landscape	Landscape	Landscape	Landscape
	Pest Control	Lease commissions	Parking Lot Maint	Lease Commissions	Travel Agent Comm	Travel Agent Comm
		Tenant Improvements	Signage	Tenant Inprovements	Security	Security
		Management Office	Lease Commissions		Franchise Fee	F&B Costs
			Tenant Improvements			Franchise Fee
	Replacement Reserve	Replacement Reserve	Replacement Reserve	Replacement Reserve	Replacement Reserve	Replacement Reser
	Total Exp	**Total Exp**	**Total Exp**	**Total Exp**	**Total Exp**	**Total Exp**
NOI	Net Operating Inc	Net Operating Inc	Net Operating Inc	Net Operating Inc	Net Operating Inc	Net Operating Inc

NOTES
1. Based on Annual Figures
2. Always Remove Depreciation, Interest, & Amortization from expenses
3. Compare 3 full years P&L plus YTD

Regardless of the categories of income and expense, value comes down to NET OPERATING INCOME

Regardless of property type, it's the annual income less expenses yields _net operating income_, the key figure used to determine value.

The following chart shows how variations in separate categories (income, expense, and debt service costs) can dramatically change cash flow and, most of all, value. A change of only 5% in all 3 categories and a slightly lower cap rate (7.5% vs 8%), bumped up separately in each column, increases the value of a $ 3,450,000 property to $4,057,200......

....an increase of $607,200 !

In short, a $100 a month net increase in monthly income adds $ 1,200 per year to the NOI. Capitalized at 8%, that's an increase in value of $15,000 ! You don't need to buy seriously troubled properties to make good money

swn book

VALUE CREATION OPPORTUNITIES CHART

				BASE YEAR	5% income Increase	PLUS 5% Expense Decrease	PLUS 5% Decrease in Debt Service	Lower Cap Rate to Target of 7.5%
Current Annual Scheduled Gross Income				$600,000	$630,000	$630,000	$630,000	
Effective Gross Income at 92% Occupancy				$552,000	$579,600	$579,600	$579,600	
Expenses at 50% of Effective Gross Income			less	$276,000	$289,800	$275,310	$275,310	
Net Operating Income				$276,000	$289,800	$304,290	$304,290	
Debt Service (1)	loan is $ 2,587,500		less	$186,160	$186,160	$186,160	$176,852	
CASH FLOW				$89,840	$103,640	$118,130	$127,438	
Capitilalized Value	8% Cap Rate			$3,450,000 Start Value	$3,622,500	$3,803,625	$3,803,625	$4,057,200 New Value
Target Cap Rate	7.50%							
Cash Flow - Return on Investment (2)					10.42%	12.02%	13.70%	14.78%

RESULT

(1) Debt Service on 75% of 8% capitalized value / 6% 30 years   Annual Return on Investment   14.78% VS   10.42%
(2) Assumes initial down payment of 25% of value : $ 862,500   Net Increase In Value $607,200
   Value Increase

WORK BOOK - BREAKOUT OF KEY FORMULA - OPPORTUNITIES

	Income
less	(Expense)
	_____
	Net Operating Income
less	**(Debt Service)**
	_____
	Cash Flow

Changes to Consider

Income	Expense	Debt
Additional Services	Tax Reduction	Longer Term
Parking Fees	Insurance Reduction	Lower Rate
Vending Machines	Higher Deductible	Discounted Leins & Loans
Laundry - Not Leased	Boiler & Machinery Insur	Renegotiate private debt
Special Services	Renegotiate Services	
Promo for Area Business	Better Tenant Screening	
Rent Sign space for others	Background checks	
Market Rents	Confirm employment	
Enforce Late Fees	Use Eviction Attorney	
Specialty Rentals	Reduce common area utilties	
Application Fees	Review utility usage	
Collect past due rents	Audit utility bills	
Upgrade tenant profile	Energy Audit	
Professional Signs	Review needs for personnel	
Enhance Street Appeal	Automate	
Web Page	Direct Mktg vs General	

Above are just some of the categories of income and expense that can possibly be raised or lowered to increase the net operating income and thereby the value and the cash flow. <u>*Improvements in operations such as these can be done on any size property, regardless of your equity ability. You can do great with only $50,000 to invest just as you can with $1million.*</u>

THE CASH COW INVESTING PLAN

Money from Nothing		Apartments
Financing Tricks	1. GETTING SEED CAPITAL	Office Buildings
Unlocking the Presentations	2. BUYING PROPERTIES	Shopping Centers
Investigating Properties	3. PARLAY to a PORTFOLIO	Warehouses
Profitable Management		Single Family Homes

STEP 1 EARN SEED CAPITAL

I found this deal in a residential MLS list, offered by a residential broker. I contracted with the owner to buy a vacant 4-plex in which she had defaulted on the mortgage, so this was a short sale (selling for less than the mortgage balance, which was in excess of $200,000). I knew that the area rents would justify an appx $225,000 value after repairs (appx $ 15,000) & fully leased: ($700/mo x 4 units x 12 x 92% occupancy = $ 30,912 less $11,000 annual expense = $19,912 NOI / .085 cap = $234,259). Using a 3rd party "proof of funds" letter, I made the offer of $105,000, cash. The owner signed the contract and after a long wait, the short sale lender countered at $110,000 which I accepted. As soon as I was under contract, I advertising the property for sale & found a cash buyer and negotiated a deal at $148,000, subject to my getting a satisfactory deal through the short sale lender. The short sale lenders approval required that I could not resell the property for 30 days. I was stuck using my corporation that I'd made the offer through. My mistake. That meant I had to buy the property and own if for 30 days before I could resell it. I closed the deal, for $ 110,000 cash using…..the end buyer's money. I arranged to give him a 1st mortgage to protect his $110,000 and a lease-option, so he could get started with the improvements right away. The option fee, $38,000 was my profit. I hind sight, I could have used an LLC to buy the deal, then just sold him the LLC or used a land trust, so even my stumbling through the more complicated method used, it worked. To date, I've never met the buyer face to face. The lease to him was "triple net", a common retail property device, which meant he was responsible for everything, so he could get started with the fix up the day I closed my purchase, with his money. The final sales documents were held by an escrow company and the sale recorded after the 30 day lease. The buyer will make slightly more than I did, but will have all the work to bring it about.

$ 38,000 MONEY FROM NOTHING – ZERO INVESTED

STEP 2   BUY A TURNAROUND PROPERTY

Let me take my 4-plex deal a step further. Let's assume we use the $ 38,000, the "money from nothing", as seed capital to find another deal and actually buy it, not flip or "wholesale" it. So, we've done step one of the plan, <u>created seed capital.</u> Lining up a "hard money lender" (no personal liability, quick funding loans), the next step is to find another troubled property like the one we flipped. Knowing the hard money lender will lend appx. 80% of the next deal, including purchase, fix up, and fees, and we set aside $8,000 for reserves, that leaves $30,000 to invest. If that represents 20% of our new investment, we have $150,000 to work with (loan and cash).

We could look for a troubled office building, strip center, warehouse, or another small apartment, or even a fixer house. Let's say we find another deal <u>to buy</u> for $ 120,000 that needs $20,000 worth of fix up. Assuming some loan fees, interest & misc costs of $ 10,000, we have capital to investment of $150,000: $120,000 in loan money and $30,000 from the seed capital. But we now own the fixed up property. A year later, we have it up and running. Using the same format at the 4 plex, we have this:

Gross Income- 4 units at $ 700/ mo x 12 months =	$ 33,600
Effective Gross Income at 90% occupancy =	$ 30,240
Less: Annual Expenses =	($9,000)
Net Operating Income	$ 21,240
Capitalized value at 8.5 % Cap Rate	$ 249,882

Now, let's get a permanent loan to pay off the hard money lender. Assuming one gets a 75% loan to value, that's $ 187,411 from the new loan. Pay off the $120,000 hard money loan and I have $ 67,411 back from the refinance, plus the $ 8,000 reserves, leaving $ 75,411 to invest, and we still own the fixed up, fully leased property.

Assume the new, permanent loan is at 7% / 30 years amortization, the mortgage payments on the $ 187,411 loan are $1,246 / mo or $14,952 / yr.

Going back to the net income:	$ 21,240
Less: New Mortgage Payments	($ 14,952)
Cash Flow	$ 6,288 / Yr

STEP 3 PARLAY INTO A PORTFOLIO

So, we've turned "nothing" into $ 38,000 and the $ 38,000 into $ 75,411 plus $6,288 per year in cash flow. Reinvest the $ 75,411 into another deal. Refinance that deal like we did the first and we are in Step 3, Parlay into a Portfolio. As one repeats the process you can assemble a portfolio of income properties, a pile of cash (eventually you may not reinvest a good part of your funds that you gain from a final refinance), plus cash flow from the properties owned.

These 3 steps are the foundation of what can be done to create lifetime cash flow and increase it with each property. It's the real estate version of what the convenience store guy did…create value, don't wait for the value to develop over time with inflation. Some call this "forced appreciation", but whatever you call it, you are creating the value by making changes that increase the net operating income and, possibly, developing a lower cap rate offering in the process. This is how you "parlay" one property into another. Your deals do not need to be big rehab or turnaround deals in which your total purchase and upgrade dollars amount to appx 75% of the target value. That's how you "refinance out" of the deal. You can buy more modest deals with less upside and the results will just take a little longer, but these properties are out there and few people understand what you've just seen here.

What follows is a summary of what the Cash Cow investor does: how one makes seed capital and then keeps properties for cash flow.

CASH COW INVESTOR - METHODS & KEY STEPS

SUMMARY

YOU ARE SEEKING	YOU GET CONTROL of PROPERTIES VIA	YOU PROFIT BY
Deals you can acquire & turnaround for appx 70% of Target Value or Control for Less Than Market Value	Options Lease Options Contract to Buy Getting a Deed	Assigning Contracts Double Closings Upgrading & Keeping for Cash Flow Reselling at Retail

STEP ONE

CALCULATE THE POSSIBLE END (FUTURE) VALUE

STEP TWO

ESTIMATE THE COSTS TO GET TO THE END VALUE
AND THE AMOUNT YOU SHOULD PAY

- Purchase Price - Try Different Ones
- Interior Improvements Estimate
- Negative Cash Flow During Carry
- Interim Loan Costs & Negative Carry
- Commissions to Agents as Applicable
- Exterior Upgrades Estimate
- Profit You Desire
- Tenant Improvement Allowance
- Tenant Incentive Bonus (commercial buildings)

STEP THREE

Make the Offer - Below Your Desired Purcahse Price From Step Two
Deterimine if you want to flip this deal or buy it and do the turnaround
Decide if any counter offer at a higher price is workable

Here's another example. A vacant 10,000 SF shopping center. Who'd want the risk of a vacant strip center, right? Let me give you a tip from mega shipping magnate Aristotle Onassis that will make this all seem far less risky. When Onassis began his career, he had no money. But that should stop no one. What he did have was chutzpah, or "brass". I'd say it was just a clever idea well executed. What he did was to locate some old oil tankers and arrange to buy them, but it was more like an option. He did not buy them outright, he only negotiated a price for which he could buy them at a bargain price. He then went to some oil company executives and, with the right to acquire the tankers in his pocket, arranged with them to lease his ships to transport their oil. With the leases in hand, he then went to a bank to arrange a loan to buy and upgrade the tankers. That's how he got started. In the same way, you can do what Onassis did or what the big boys who build skyscrapers do to get the financing to build their buildings. They get commitments from enough tenants (pre-leasing) to make the proposed building economically viable on paper. Then they go to the bank to get the money to build the property with these lease commitments in hand. With a commercial property like our shopping center, one could offer a bonus, in addition to a nice build out of the vacant space, to come to this center. That bonus might include your paying to market their specific business in the new location or even cash, subject to your getting it leased up and refinanced or sold when full. There are lists of tenants available from various services, or go to a commercial leasing broker, so the pieces of the puzzle exist. Even a small, vacant office building suitable for one tenant could be a candidate. Here's how to calculate a shopping center deal. Most deals you come across will be partially occupied, giving you some income when you get started, but the idea is the same. <u>These are the three steps:</u>

1. Compute the end or target value possible using area rents and cap rates.
2. Estimate the costs to get it from where it is to the target operation. Include your desired profit, financing costs, and reserves in the list.
3. You now have an offering price. Try for even lower on your initial offer.

If you get a response price that's acceptable, assign the deal or buy it, remembering how Onassis hedged his bet by having some prospective lease income lined up. In same way, you do some pre-leasing. If you get an unacceptable counter offer that creates too much risk or too little profit, walk away. But come back in 30 days and then 60 days, etc. Time and circumstance do change people's willingness to deal.

Vacant Strip Shopping Center – 10,000 SF

FIRST - Determine Target (End) Value

$15 psf / yr market rents x 10K sf = $ 150,000 / yr at full occupancy	
Effective Gross Income at 92% Occupancy	$ 138,700
Less Expenses at 35% of gross	- ($ 48,300)
Net Operating Income	$ 89,700
Cap Rate 8.5% (divide NOI by .085)	**$ 1,055,294**
	END VALUE

Determine & Subtract Estimated Costs

SECOND

Tenant Build Out Allowance	$ 140,000	($14 x 10 k sf)
Estimated Repairs	$ 60,000	
Financing 5% of $750 K	$ 37,500	
Commissions	$ 30,240	(9K x 4 yrs x $14 x 6%)
Misc & Reserves	$ 25,000	
Tenant Incentives	$ 210,000	est 7 tenant at $ 30 k avg
Total Appx Cost	$ 502,740	

To get some of these costs, like repairs, just break down the individual needs, like signage, parking lot striping, etc then, if you don't get bids, check out Youtube or just go on line to find out appx costs for each requirement.

What to Offer

THIRD

        Target Value $ 1,055,294
        Less Costs   ($ 502,740)
        Balance $ 552,554   for Profit and Purchase Offer

Example $ 325,000 purchase yields $ 227,554 PROFIT

A $ 227,554 Profit !

<u>Between fully leased, high priced properties and completely vacant properties like this example, there are partially leased or poorly managed properties or properties in need of repair, or any combination of these issues, that are hugely profitable. These are the properties on which the Cash Cow investor will focus. One property can serve to generate seed capital to then buy your first property & it can then be used, after refinance, to finance the purchase of others, while you keep the ones you've bought, creating a cash flow for life.</u>

Here are the key steps in determining what to offer and how to profit from a property operating below it's potential. This is the domain of the Cash Cow investor.

START WITH THE END-TARGET VALUE & WORK BACK

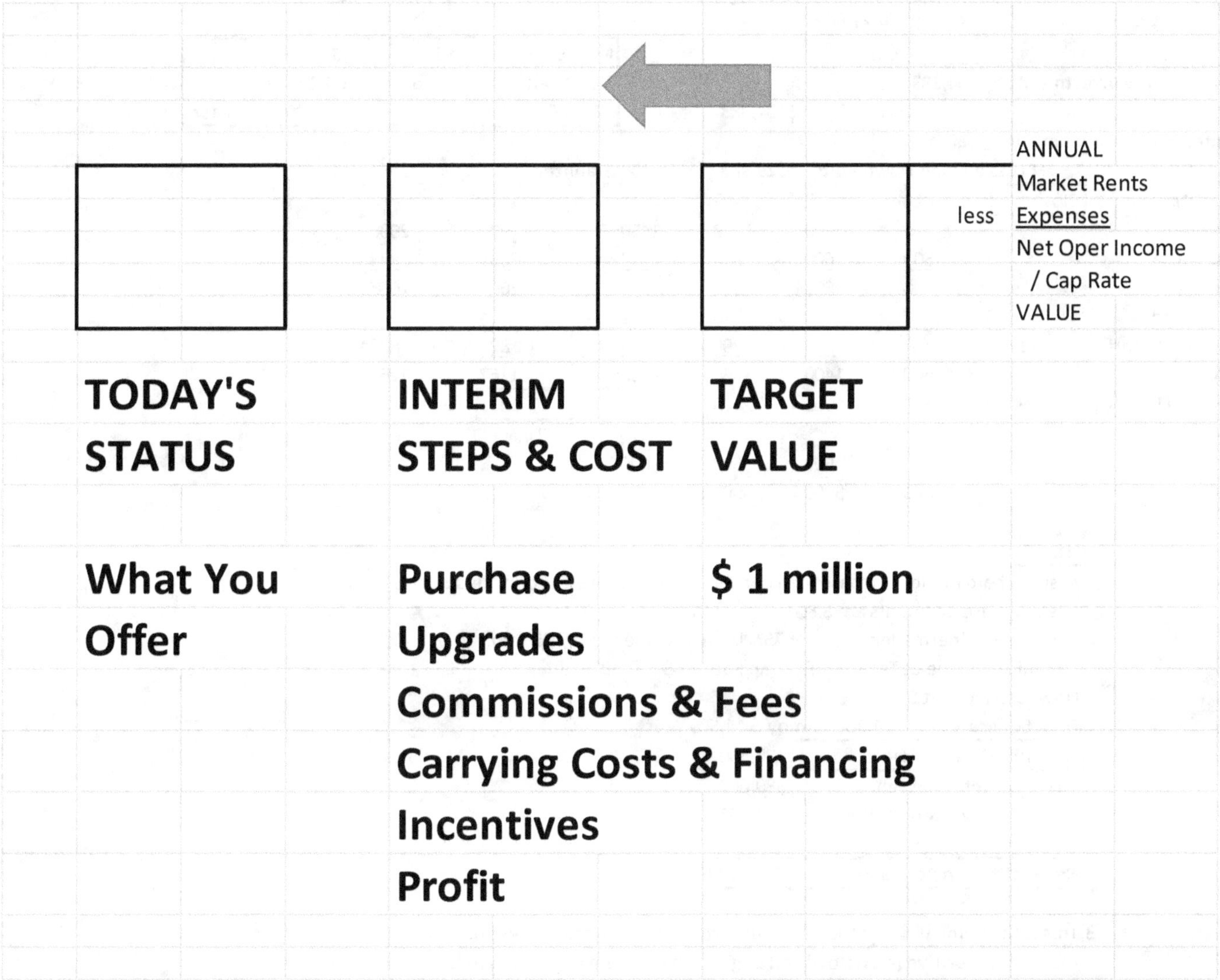

☐	☐	☐	ANNUAL Market Rents less Expenses Net Oper Income / Cap Rate VALUE
TODAY'S STATUS	**INTERIM STEPS & COST**	**TARGET VALUE**	
What You Offer	Purchase Upgrades Commissions & Fees Carrying Costs & Financing Incentives Profit	$ 1 million	

The next chart shows more detail and a simple way to lay out an overall investment plan on one sheet. This assumes the lease up of a 4 plex, includes the negative cash flow during lease up and upgrades, then a resale at the end. With only 4 units, the turnaround could be in months. But this same layout can apply to a much bigger property of any type and the time line may be for one or two years. But the idea is the same. Get out your Excel sheet! I go over charts like these in the audio recordings included in the Cash Cow Home Study Course: see the back of this book. Remember, learning things like this will put you in a rare category to be self-sufficient, which most people will never bother to do.

workbook **Stages of A Turnaround** SAMPLE 4-PLEX

PURCHASE		INTERIM		TARGET VALUE			
		$25,000	Down Pmt	$225,000	target		Annual Operation
	$105,000	$1,200	closing costs	Income	$34,800	4 x $725 mo x 12	
		$15,000	fix up & repair costs	Eff Gross Inc	$31,320	90% occupancy	
$25,000	Down	$2,400	borrowed funds cost	less: Expense	$10,000	per year	
$80,000	Loan	$1,800	marketing costs	Net Op Income	$21,320		
		$2,000	fees and misc	Debt Service	$14,500	75% LTV (2)	
		$2,583	negative operating costs	Cash Flow	$6,820	per year	
		$5,000	reserve				
				New Equity Created		$37,500	
Total Equity Investment		$54,983		Net Profit From Refinance		$52,517 (4)	
		Total Deal	$134,983	Plus Cash Flow		$6,820	per year
Interim Loan Amount (1)		$80,000					
		Costs beyond Down Pmt	$29,983	Stablized			

OPERATIONS	Closing	Month 1	2	3	4	5	6
Income / mo		0	0	0	1450	2900	2900
Expense Mo		500	600	800	833	833	833
Net Income		-500	-600	-800	617	2067	2067
units occupied		0	0	0	2	4	4
Debt Service (interim loan) (1)		800	800	800	800	800	800
Cash Flow		-500	-1400	-1600	-183	1267	1267
Cumm Cash Flow - Operations		-500	-1900	-2400	-2583	-1316	-49
						TURNS (3)	
Marketing			600	600	600		
Repairs		5000	5000	5000			

NOTES

1 Assume hard money purchase loan of $80,000 at 12% interest only plus 3% up front fee.
   Debt service payments are $800 per month

2 Assume end (permanent) loan of 75% Loan to Value at 6% / 25 years
   Capitalized Value at Target/ 8.5% Cap Rate --- $250,000 Value
   New loan amount $187,500.
   Debt Service $1,208.27 mo / $14,500 Year

NEW PERMANENT LOAN		$187,500
Less	Interim Loan	$80,000
less	Invested Capital	$54,983
Net Profit From Refinance		$52,517

3 This is the point at which the maximum accumulative negative loss occurs
   Month 5, is positive (cash flow) and begins repaying the cummulative loss.

4 This returns 89.9% of original investment.
   If you assume the investment remaining of $5,666 is
     now generating $6,820 in cash flow, that's 120 % per year on
     this remaining amount.
   You also have the net of refinance to parlay into another deal.

CASH COW INVESTING APPLIED

Let me further explain what a cash cow investment looks like vs a typical investment. In working with clients over the last 37 years, one thing stood out. Those who did exceptionally well bought troubled properties at wholesale. Those who did not, paid retail. "Troubled" is a broad term but it's a property that allows for a very large upside profit. There are, of course, many profitable situations in between these extremes.

One of my early brokerage transactions was a 76 unit apartment. The owner had inherited it from his parents and was clueless about running it. It was in a decent location, but it was run down and the tenant profile was not very good (lots of cars in the parking lot during normal work hours), and the occupancy was low. The place was free of debt, thankfully, but at 60% occupancy if one needs all the rent money just to break even, that's a bad situation. As I was new to the business, even I did't see much hope. I had the same thinking that gets many investors in trouble: if it's not new or at least in great shape, and occupancy was bad, who'd want it? The savior did arrive in the guise of a quiet spoken man dressed like a day laborer. Within 10 days of our meeting, we closed the sale for $750,000 cash. Within 60 days, the place looked much better and occupancy was near 90%. Within that few months, I now estimate that "cash cow" buyer had created a $2 million asset from his $750,000 purchase. Because he did not put a loan on it, he'd paid cash, his cash flow was the net operation income, or appx $ 200,000 a year or $16,666 a month. That's about 26% per annum return on his investment, maybe a little less after fix up costs. As this property was added to his portfolio of other high cash flow properties, you can now see where he got the $750,000 to buy this one.

Now, this investor, Darby Suiter, became a friend for the next 25 years and I helped him buy a lot more properties. When he passed away a couple of years ago, after having sold off all his holdings, he left cash and stocks worth appx $50 million according to his attorney.

The non-cash cow investor is the one who'd buy the fixed up, 92% occupancy property from the cash cow investor. But, where does one go from there? There's limited upside. The big money has been earned by the cash cow investor. My friend was on the end game of the cash cow plan. He'd started small, then had enough cash flow to invest and create even more cash flow (step 3 of the plan). Learning the "cash cow investing" plan is what this book is about.

Keys to Cash Cow Investing
Minimal or no out of pocket investment to start. Earn seed capital.
Focus on properties with excellent upside revenue potential due to existing below market rents, mismanagement, low occupancy, high expenses, condition issues or any combination of these.
Dealing with motivated-to-sell owners.
Finding a low risk situation that may look high risk to the uninformed
Buying such that you can structure an opportunity to return all your invested capital and, perhaps, part of your profit too upon refinancing, once the property operation is stabilized.

YOU ARE SEEKING UNDER PERFORMING or "VALUE ADDED" PROPERTIES IN ORDER TO "CREATE VALUE" THROUGH YOUR EFFORTS. TO RAISE SEED CAPITAL, SELL THIS OPPORTUNITY. PROPERTIES IN GOOD CONDITION BUT WITH FINANCIAL ISSUES ALSO WORK TO EARN SEED CAPITAL. YOU THEN USE THE SEED CAPITAL TO BUY THESE VALUE ADDED PROPERTIES TO KEEP & USE AS A SOURCE, UPON REFINANCING, TO BUY OTHERS AND RETAIN THEIR CASH FLOW.

What follows is the actual flyer I used to market the 4 plex (which is detailed in the following "Earn Seed Capital" portion of the Cash Cow investing plan) in which I made $38,000 with zero risk or investment. A few details are altered but the math is as offered.

I don't think the buyer understood all this, but he got a good deal regardless.

STEAL THIS 4 PLEX FOR SOLID CASH FLOW
CARLISLE / COMANCHE NE AREA
$ 160,000 Price + $15 K Upgrades : $ 270,000 ASSET

LARGE UNITS 4-PLEX

Needs cabinets and clean up. High Visability.

Large Units 3 two Bedroom 1 one Bedroom

UNITS VACANT

Contact Scott for Proforma Details

propertytrust@xxxx.com

or call xxx-xxx-xxx ext xxx

* PROFORMA

GROSS SCHEDULED INCOME		$ 32,820
EFFECTIVE GROSS (92% Occ)		$ 30,194
LESS: EXPENSES		($ 11,222)
Net Operating Income		$18,972
Capitalized Value	6%	$ 316,207
	7%	$ 271,034
	8%	$ 237,155

Refinance 75% of Value, assume $ 250,000, After upgrades an full occupancy, $ 187,500 loan. Loan <u>Constant</u> of 6.5% for debt service of $12,187 per year.   CASH FLOW $ 6,875 / yr

Remaining Cash Invested —ZERO
Created Net Equity - $ 62,500 to $ 83,500

FULL OPERATIONAL DETAILS UPON REQUEST

HARD MONEY LOAN AVAILABLE FOR 75% of AFTER REPAIR VALUE: APPX 15% EQUITY REQUIRED– Appx $ 30K

Offeree is an investor & the contracted purchaser. Final price subject to short sale in process.

THE FALLACY that BIG REWARDS REQUIRE BIG RISK

In their landmark book, From Predators to Icons , French scholars Michel Villette and Catherine Vullermot researched the details of the business transactions done by some of the most well-known, mega-successful investors in the world, in various businesses. What they discovered was that, contrary to public perception, they DO NOT take big risks. Not at all. They look for huge profit potential with minimal risk.

Let's take one as an example, Ted Turner, founder of CNN. Ted inherited a decently operating bill board business in Atlanta from his father. In time, he decided he wanted to get into the television business and focused on buying local WJRJ, a UHF channel (you needed a special antenna to receive it). It was losing about $500,000 a year. He arranged to buy it with stock from his company, so zero cash down. Rather than just buy it and hope for the best, which would have been a big risk, he went to NBC to arrange to buy programs that their affiliates were not picking up, which they were allowed to sell to anyone. After getting a deal for 4 programs, Turner then posted on many of his billboard, "NBC MOVES TO CHANNEL 17 !". Viewership increased, ad revenues did too, and by the end of year three he netted $1million from the once failing channel. Hardly high risk. Deals like this, low risk high reward, one after another, created his empire.

A more recent example is John Paulson. A Wall Street money manager, around 2005 Paulson became curious about the housing market. Those where the days of an increasing number of home loans in which anyone who could fog up a mirror could get one. The first thing he did was to do a study of what was really going on. Seeing that this dizzying market of near endless building and house flipping could not continue, he looked for a way to safely capitalize on a market he was certain would eventually crash. What he did was to start buying the quasi-insurance policies known as credit default swaps. These "swaps" insured investors from loss if the packages of mortgages they bought went south and the borrowers defaulted. No one of Wall Street believed that could ever happen, at least in quantity. They were laughing at Paulson who was buying $100 million policies for about 10 cents on the dollar of insurance value, making the policy payments, all in the hopes the market would crash and he'd make a fortune. If the market had not crashed, he'd be out the money he'd been paying out monthly for policies on which he'd never collect. The movie, The Big Short, chronicles his adventure and some nail biting periods he'd have to go back to his investors for more money to keep borrowing the money to keep pay the premiums. When the market stated crashing in 2008, he made $1.25 billion in one morning alone. Overall, he and his partners made about $5 billion profit on an investment of a very small fraction of that.

If you want to see the condensed version of this study, it really is fascinating, see author Malcom Gladwell's article, *The Sure Thing*, at his web site www.Gladwell.com. From my own experience, I can tell you there is one thing I've seen over and over with astute investors; their big payoff deals are low investment, high return. I'm not suggesting this extreme end of the spectrum is for everyone, but a very wide range of excellent returns on investment exists in small property real estate, but risk can be reduced.

Donald Trump, in his book, <u>The Art of the Deal</u>, reveals that when he was buying the Bonwit Teller building to tear it down and put up what is now Trump Tower, Bonwit still wanted a presence in his new building, albeit only about 25% of the space they were giving up. <u>Trump negotiated a lease with Bonwit that virtually paid his expected mortgage payment on the loan he was getting to build the tower!</u> By the way, it's routine that when a developer puts up a big commercial property, pre-leasing to cover most of the cost of the risk component of the venture is the way it's done.

Jerry J. Moore, whom you'll be introduced to further on, who bought near vacant neighborhood shopping centers *already had his "usual suspects" ready to lease* after he bought the centers for pennies on the dollar. His bargain purchases allowed him to give them bargain rents.

Shipping magnate Aristotle Onassis, who married Jackie Kennedy, began his career by getting options to buy old oil tankers, then he got contracts from big oil companies to lease them before making the purchases, as noted earlier. Those leases allowed him to borrow the money to buy the tankers. He also bought half interest in Monte Carlo from Prince Rainer when it was an unknown backwater, then brought in all his movie star friends to give it glamor and put it on the map. Now you can't get even get a slot in the harbor for a yacht smaller than 150 feet in length. Small risk, big reward.

The lesson of all this is that one can minimize risk on even the most modest, small property deal. By small, I'm suggesting apartments from 4 to 50 units and commercial buildings from 2,000 SF to 20,000 SF. <u>The business, regardless of property size, is the same.</u>

So, I ask you, if you started with nothing and earned, say $60,000 doing some of the seed capital steps (options, assignments, etc) then invested that money in a deal, even if it tanked and you lost most of it, are you really worse off? Not really. You've only invested money from nothing you earned by knowledge, not risk.

BEAUTIFUL PROPERTIES CAN WORK TOO

Now, you don't need to find fixer properties to earn seed capital money. Here's an example of a deal I did with a beautiful property that was only troubled financially. A little back ground first.

One of the ways many name brand retail stores keep their cash flow going in order to expand is to sell their properties and lease them back long term. Alternatively, a building developer actually builds the building for them and this developer owns the building. He gets the financing arranged to build it with the lease from the financially solid tenant in hand. Remember Onassis and his oil company leases? Other times, a company owned store will sell their existing building and lease it back long term. All this is usually under the arrangement called a *sale lease back*. These deals are usually arranged as a triple net lease (NNN lease). This means the tenant will pay all costs associated with the building (taxes, insurances, utilities, building maintenance, etc) and the landlord, owner, gets a dependable rent check every month. There are variations on whether landlord or tenant pay certain expenses, but true NNN deals are expense free to the owner. These are highly desirable properties. Leases can often run for an initial term of 10 years or more with the right of tenant to renew the lease in increments for many years beyond this, like for 4 five year options after the initial term. But you don't' have to be Walmart, Auto Zone, Dollar General, a US post office, or Home Depot to get someone interested in owning your building subject to you leasing it.

Many Well Known Firms Lease Their Buildings and Investors Own Them.

SEED CAPITAL CAN BE MADE WITH ATTRACTIVE PROPERTIES TOO, NOT JUST FIXERS, IN THE COMMERCIAL REAL ESTATE WORLD. HERE'S AN EXAMPLE. Here I applied the simple triple net concept.

Medical Office Condo

A medical group contacted me in response to a letter I sent out to owners of properties that appeared on a defaulted loans list. It seems that during the downturn, their specialty was an elective matter, so their business had dropped off in a big way. They were behind in mortgage payments. They'd paid appx $470,400 for the property then put in about $411,600 in permanent improvements to what was likely an empty shell of a building.

They financed about $750,000 of this $882,000 cost. Their space was 2,940 SF which they owned. It was part of an office condo complex. Looking at some area rents the top of the market appeared to be about $ 18 psf, with the tenants paying much of the building costs, but this was in multi-tenant offices, not individual condos. Not a lot to draw from but it was not out of line with high end office rents in a broader area in the city. This property was on the outskirts.

So this is the rate I used; a market rent of $ 18 psf / yr NNN (tenant paying all costs of upkeep, taxes, insurance, utilities, and the association fees which covered outside upkeep, structure and roof. I knew smaller triple net deals, under $ 2 million were hard to find and what few were offered were near or below 8% cap rate, offering an 8% all cash purchase annual return from the rent payments.

With that in mind coupled with the fact that my lease back tenants were coming out of a challenging period, I decided to use a 9% cap rate to establish value and offer this return to the market.

2,940 SF x $18 = $ 52,980 yr ($ 4,415 mo rent) - This is the NOI

Capitalize NOI at 9% - My Established Value $ 589,000

The flyer I created, noted on next page was put on www.Loopnet.com. The result? Within 4 days I received a letter of intent from an investor, who was also a real estate agent and an attorney, investing family money. As we waited out the short sale lender for a response to my contract price with the owner, I recall it being about $525,000 we worked out the details of the lease with the tenants. Some other court issues regarding bankruptcy of the legal entity in which the doctors held the building had to be resolved so more time elapsed. In the end, we redid my contract between the end buyer and the doctor tenants and I negotiated getting $25,000 from the buyer for my position. The buyer did pay all cash, no loan needed and receives a check each month, with scheduled in the future on the 10 year lease, earning him 9% return, to start, on his investment. Money from nothing on my part.

WESTERN DENTAL BUILDING

TRIPLE NET LEASE

9 % Cap Rate

3201 San Felipe Rd—Houston, TX

Leverage Return— 10% per annum*

Price $ 589,000.oo

Appx 2,950 SF Office Condo Project

Proposed 5 Year Term w/ 2 five year renewal options—15 Yr total

$ 4,415 Mo Lease with CPI Increases

Just north of I-10 between Hwy 303 to the west and Hwy 101 to the east.

Contact **F. Scott Tonges** - PropertyTrust@Frontier.net

713-000-000   / AGENTS WELCOME

Offeree is investor/optionee

Tenant will lease back and pays all costs of building operation and upkeep.

* Assumes $147,250 down (25%) and loan of $441,750 at 7.25% interest / 25 year amorizatioin—Loan Payments $ 3,193 mo.

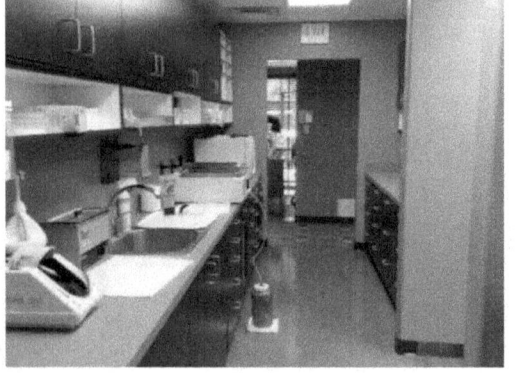

DISTANCE INVESTING

With the internet today, and video communication as close as your cell phone, you are not confined to investing in your own back yard, though it's always worth checking out. With Google Maps you can virtually "drive" a neighborhood. With some modest assistance on the other end, you can pay someone to handle routine paper shuffling for leases and contracts, an attorney is a good idea to handle that, and if someone needs to open a space to show a prospect, it's $12 an hour work. In the same way I had to expand my mind to become an investor, not just a broker, I had to do the same thing to "get out of town". When you are earning seed capital, you don't need to go look at a property. You really can do deals without ever having to meet face to face with a buyer or seller or see the property yourself. If you're not the end buyer, the location and the condition of the roof are not your concern.

Once you have the seed capital and plan to invest, how difficult or costly can it be to catch a quick flight, have one overnight stay to see the deal you intend to buy, and also meet with contractors you've lined up in advance, the management firm you plan to hire, then set up a webcast for future, even daily tracking of what may need to be done? To quote the motto of a friend who's a hotel developer, *"How hard can it be?"* If you can go to Youtube and learn the basic tools and methods you need to paint a room or a house, install a roof vent, and about every other skill on the planet, you can do the same to fill in many of the blanks you may be concerned about in handling any property challenge. The same holds for the details of real estate investing. Most of the key things you want to know or do are farmed out to others, too; lawyers can handle lease forms and contracts, contractors handle repairs and fix ups, mangers deal with tenants. You're the director of you own movie and you leave all the details to professionals.

Where should you invest? A good start is in growing communities. You can get on line maps that show counties where people are moving, to and from, and that's a good start. Within a neighborhood, an area banker can tell you a lot about what's going on. Who lives in a given neighborhood? Check out a local grocery store on a Saturday afternoon.

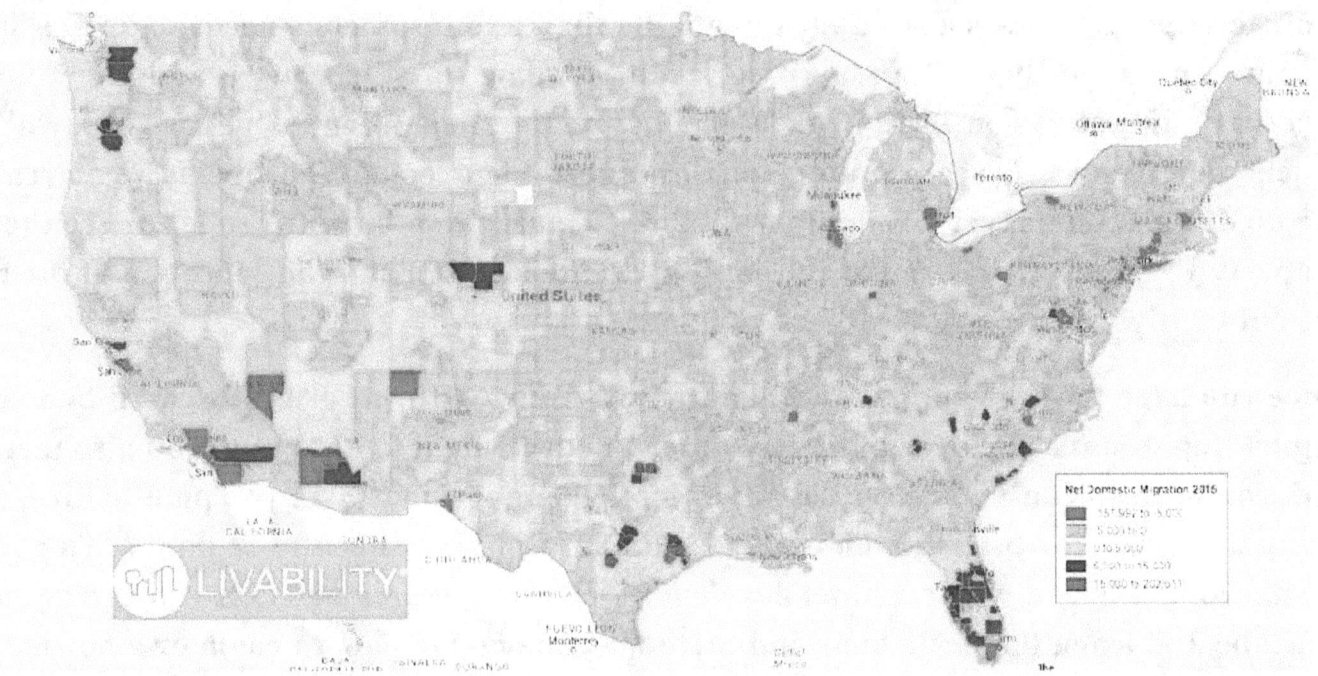

You can Google "where are people moving?" to get a map like this on line. It shows the counties that are gaining or losing population or staying the same, across the country. This is very good to know. It's tough to make money where demand is decreasing.

BASIC INVESTING VS CASH COW INVESTING

What I've done in the next two charts is to compare a 5 year hold, then sale, on two 40 unit apartments. The first one (Basic Investment) is bought with market rents in place and at 90% occupancy. I then assumed rents and expenses rose each year by 2% percent as noted, then the property was sold at the end of year 5, sales costs are deducted and the pay down of the original loan was also included. It shows an overall, average annual return on the original investment of 20.09%. This is what I call an inflation investment or a "retail" or "market" deal. It's fine for many investors, and maybe you are one of them.

In the next chart (Turnaround Investment Sample) I assume the purchase of a Cash Cow type deal. It's only 70% occupied so a bit of negotiation on price is assumed. I further assume some costs are involved to improve the property to get the rents to market rates. A more expensive, rate wise, short term, hard money loan is in place upon purchase as this is a turnaround deal. It will be replaced with a permanent, long term, less expensive loan. The property is stabilized by the end of year 2 and refinanced at that time. The new, less expensive permanent loan is eventually put on the property, so you see the debt service drops.

The REFINANCE ON THIS 2nd PROPERTY RETURNS THE ORIGINAL INVESMENT PLUS PART OF THE INCREASED VALUE. YOU CAN KEEP THIS PROPERTY AND IT'S CASH FLOW FOR PERMANENT INCOME IF YOU DESIRE. You now have funds to go buy another property on which to do the same thing.

Though I show an average annual return on the original investment, your cash flow could continue with property 2 in which you have no remaining investment at all. This is Cash Cow Investing. Even if you sold the property as the illustration assumes, it's a great return on investment…44.8% vs 20% and the option of keeping it with no investment left in it. These are AVERAGE ANNUAL RETURNS.

CHART 1 – "BASIC INVESTING" is INFLATION INVESTING

CHART 2 - "TURN AROUND INVESTMENT" is CASH COW INVESTING

Again, in chart two, 100% of the invested capital is returned & the property can be kept for cash flow. You can reinvest the returned funds. This is how you "parlay" your investment. It's not for everyone, but it's one of 5 general ranges of opportunities with income properties. You don't need a mess of a property to make progress to increase your passive income.

BASIC INVESTMENT

40 Unit Property

	CURRENT				5 YEARS OUT
	Assume 5 Year Hold with 2% Inflation on Rents & Expenses/yr				

OPERATIONS

	Buy Year 1	Year 2	Year 3	Year 4	Year 5
INCOME Rent/Month/Unit	$625	$638	$650	$663	$677
Units	x 40				
Scheduled Gross Income / Yr	$300,000	$306,000	$312,120	$318,362	$324,730
Occupancy	90%	90%	90%	90%	90%
Effective Gross Income / Year	$270,000	$275,400	$280,908	$286,526	$292,257
Less **EXPENSES**					
48% of EGI	$129,600	$132,192	$134,836	$137,533	$140,283
Net Operating Income NOI	$140,400	$143,208	$146,072	$148,994	$151,973
Debt Service	$94,799	$94,799	$94,799	$94,799	$94,799
Cash Flow	$45,601	$48,409	$51,273	$54,195	$57,174
Capitalize Value					
9 % Cap Rate	$1,560,000	$1,591,200	$1,623,024	$1,655,484	$1,688,594

INVESTMENT SUMMARY

ASSUMPTIONS

	PURCHASE			SALE	
Purchase Price	$1,560,000		Sale Price	$1,688,594
25 % Down	$390,000	less	Costs 5%	$84,430
Mortgage *	$1,170,000	less	Mtg Balance	$1,059,577
			Gross Profit	$544,587
* Debt Service 6.5% / 25 Yrs	plus	5 Yr Cash Flo	$256,652
Payments $ 7,899.92 / mo	less	Down Pmt	$390,000
			Net Profit	$411,240
			Avg Ann Return on Down Payment	$82,247.94
			As Percent of Down Pmt	**21.09%**

TURNAROUND INVESTMENT SAMPLE

40 Unit Property

CURRENT | | | | | 5 YEARS OUT

Assume 5 Year Hold with 2% Inflation on Rents & Expenses/yr

OPERATIONS

	Buy Year 1	Year 2	Year 3	Year 4	Year 5
INCOME Rent/Month/Unit	$550	$638	$650	$663	$677
Units	x 40				
Scheduled Gross Income / Yr	$264,000	$306,240	$312,000	$318,240	$324,960
Occupancy	70%	80%	90%	90%	90%
Effective Gross Income / Year	$184,800	$244,992	$280,800	$286,416	$292,464
Less **EXPENSES**					
48% of EGI	$100,000	$117,596	$134,784	$137,480	$140,383
Net Operating Income NOI	$84,800	$127,396	$146,016	$148,936	$152,081
Debt Service	$111,600	$111,600	$94,799	$94,799	$94,799
Cash Flow	($26,800)	$15,796	$51,217	$54,137	$57,282
Capital Costs $3500 / unit	$140,000				
Total Cost: Purch + Cap Costs	$1,240,000				
Cash Flow for Yr w Cap Costs	($166,800)				
Capitalize Value					
9 % Cap Rate	Negotiated	Stablization	$1,622,400	$1,654,848	$1,689,792

INVESTMENT SUMMARY

ASSUMPTIONS

	PURCHASE			SALE	
Purchase Price	$1,100,000	Negotiated		Sale Price	$1,689,792
Down - 25 % Of Total Costs	$275,000		less	Costs 5%	$84,490
Two Yr Interim Loan (1)	$930,000		less	Mtg Balance	$1,152,401
Year 3 Perm Loan (2)	$1,216,800			Gross Profit	$452,901
			plus	Net of Refin	$286,800
			plus	5 Yr Cash Flow	$151,632
75% if Total Costs (1)	12 % Interest Only		less	Down Pmt	$275,000
Funded first of Yr 3 (2)	Debt Service 6.5% / 25 Yrs			Net Profit	$616,334
	Payments $7,899.92 / mo	Avg Ann Return			
	75% of Value			on Down Payment	$123,267
				As Percent of Down Pmt	44.82%

Loan Fees omitted
Interim loan of 75% of purchase and upgrade costs
Refinance at end of year 3 and recoup much of original investment

No Remaining Investment After Refinance

HOW TO UNRAVEL AN OFFERING

Next is a real world example of a small shopping center noted earlier. The tenants were all on month-to-month leases. That's what scared off most investors. The plan was to give a modest financial inducement to the tenants to sign 2, 3, or 4 year leases, prior to closing. They would gain pre-set increases each of year. This gives them and the investor some security and stabilization. This owner owed appx. $450,000 and only wanted appx $35,000 down on a $500,000 price, just to pay the closing costs and be done with it. Assuming a 3 year hold (see lower right summary block) then resale, an investment with generous reserves totaling _$80,000 generates a total return on investment of 215% or an average annual return of 71.6% per annum._ No fix up needed on this nicely kept property. See the details on the next page on each area of the projection. It will show you a good way to lay out and understand any income property.

space	Unit No	SHOPPING CENTER SAMPLE	Current Monthly	Current Annual	NEW LEASES PROPOSED Year 1 monthly	Year 1 Annual	Year 2 Monthly	Year 2 Monthly	Year 3 Monthly	Year 3 Annual			
1	101	1 tenant	700		750		800		900		Center 8,383 SF		
2&3	102,103	2 Tenants	1258		1400		1500		1600		11 Spaces / Avg 762 SF each		
4	104,104	2 tenants	615		715		775		800				
5	105	1 tenant	500		600		700		800				
6	106	VACANT	0								ASSUMES 90% OCCUPANCY		
7	107	2 tenants	560		660		725		800				
8	108	1 tenant	661		700		750		800				
9	109	1 tenant	600		700		725		800				
10	110	1 tenant	560		650		725		800				
11	111	1 tenant	630		625		725		800				
			current plus		Yr 1 leases		Yr 2 leases		Year 3 leases				
			6084	73008	6800	81600	7425	89100	8100	97200	Down	$35,000	
	Expenses	Taxes	per seller	10200		10506		10821		11146	Incentives	$15,000	
		Insurance	per seller	1800		1854		1910		1967	Misc	$7,500	
		Trash	per seller	1928		1985.84		2045		2107	Legal	$2,500	
		Electric	per seller	5100		5253		5411		5573	Reserves	$20,000	
		Gas	per seller	1702		1753.06		1806		1860			
		Water	per seller	734		756		779		802	Invest	$80,000	
		Sewer	per seller	2700		2781		2864		2950			
		Ads		500		515		530		546	less deposits received		
		Accounting		500		515		530		546	asssume 6/6.5/7% loan rate		
		Legal		1200		1236		1273		1311			
		Snow		500		515		530		546	3 Years Hold then resale		
		Repairs		1200		1236		1273		1311			
		Signage		1500		1545		1591		1639	Cash Flow		ROI
		Plumbing		1200		1236		1273		1311	Yr 1	$11,101	13.88%
		Carpets+		1500		1545		1591		1639	Yr 2	$15,678	19.60%
		Hardware		500		515		530		546	Yr 3	$20,719	25.90%
		HVAC		500		515		530		546	Resale end year 3		
		Mgt		1200		1236		1273		1311	sale	$701,832	
		Misc		1500		1545		1591		1639	minus loan bal	$448,000	
	Total Exp			35964		37043	45%	38154	43%	39299	minus 7% fees	$49,128	
	NOI			$37,044		$44,557		$50,946		$57,901	sale net	$204,704	
	DS			37128 ??		33456		35268		37182	plus 3 yr CF	$47,498	
	CF			-$84		$11,101		$15,678		$20,719	Total ROI	$252,202	
	Cap Value 8.25%			$449,018		$540,086		$617,525		$701,832	Net ROI	$172,202	215.25%

In the preceding shopping center sample, here's how it's done. Each tenant was listed and their current rents noted. This is to establish what you are buying: it's all about "today". You first want to know what you are walking in to. You can also do projections on a month to month basis if you want more details for more quickly changing rents, costs, and capital improvements. We're just trying to get the big picture to start on a center that's in good shape. We plan to sign up new leases for year one with the current tenants, to get them, slowly, say over 3 years, up to a market rate.

The first column ("current monthly") is totaled, then annualized. At the bottom of this first column you input the estimated annual costs as closely and conservatively as possible. Next, we make assumptions of increased rents each year, starting year one of ownership, then increase those and the expenses on into years 2 and 3.

For each column, at the bottom, we apply a cap rate to estimate the value we've created by increased net operating income. In the lower right block, we sell the center at the end of year 3 of ownership. We note the sales price, subtract the loan balance at that time, deduct the costs of sale, add in the 3 years of expected cash flow, and that leaves a gross profit. From that, we subtract the invested capital, $80,000 (I assumed we used up the reserves). That yields an overall return on investment (the money made on top of the investment) of $172,202 or 215.25%. To get an overall average over 3 years, divide by three. At 71.75% per year, that's a great deal.

In the next chart, I show you a very general range of possible investment returns. In the first two, maybe number 3 as well in some cases, I only assume your annual return without resale. It's cash flow. Resale can improve the overall return on investment, as noted in the two 40 unit apartment samples and the one I just explained.

As you get into areas 4 and 5, the 100% and up return can be achieved by resale or refinance. You have the opportunity, the option actually, to refund most or all of your investment and still keep the property and the cash flow. It's can often be as much as 12% per annum calculated on the original investment (but that investment is fully refunded via the refinance).

You have created new value, and this could be offered to the market as an investment like the one in the first box, as a "retail" or "market value" offering. But as you already have all your investment back, keeping this passive cash flow is the target I encourage you to consider.

LIFETIME PASSIVE INCOME

Property Types

Office / Apartment / Retail / Warehouse / Hybrids / Lodging / Limited Residential

Plans

Stage One Investors— Start without Cash or Credit / A 5 Year Plan to develop

      $75,000 / Yr Passive Income
      $ 1 million net worth
      $ 250,000 cash from last refinance   (Get the Home Study Course)

Stage Two Investors - Currently have investments in any asset type, stocks, etc
      Maximize & Expand Cash Flow by Repositioning Assets
      Diversify and/ or Develop a Portfolio

Stage Three Investors—Experienced Income Property Owners / Passive or Active
      Diversify to other property types
      Acquire additional properties

The 5 General Investing Options / Single or Multi-Tenant

1. **Triple Net:** National/Regional Credit Tenants - zero upkeep or costs to investor
      7% to 11% Secure Annual Returns

2. **Market Value investments** / Well Maintained Properties
      12% & Up Annual Returns on Investment

3. **Upside Investments** / Rent & Operations Improvements
      15% to 20% Annual Returns

4. **Cosmetic Upgrade & Operational Improvements**
      25% to 50% Avg annual Returns

5. **Full Upgrade Properties**
      100% Return (upon refinance) and keep the cash flow

These labels are my own, not any official or general industry standard. There is none.

A Cash Cow Investor Gallery

<u>These opportunities can work on any size income property.</u> At the far end, I call the process *<u>Cash Cow investing.</u>* At this extreme, it allows you to recycle most or all of a single investment from one property to the next, keeping the cash flow from each property as you go. Here are some who've done it for years.

You may be wondering if this Cash Cow concept is all a fantasy. Noted below are some of the true Cash Cow investors I've had the pleasure of working with and learning from. Sadly, all are gone, having passed away very recently, in their 80's but working up until then. But what they did is timeless and what I learned from them, and others, and now pass on to you and help investors achieve high return on their investments. What these gentlemen did formed much the foundation of my Cash Cow education.

George Ablah - George's focus was buying and upgrading defunct distribution warehouses but he'd buy anything that was a good deal. My first visit with George was on board his $12 million Gulf Stream jet which included a $ 4 million sculpture collection built into custom niches on the plane. One of his greatest deals was to buy all 850 Chrysler dealerships in America when the company was going under (the first time) for $130 million cash. Some months later, the chairman, Lee Iacocca, got a government bailout loan, so needed dealerships again. When Lee bought back the remainder George had not sold off, about half the portfolio, he paid George…$130 million for the remainder. George and his wife, Virginia, was as generous with their time & advice as they with their success, donating art and money to public institutions and colleges. We talked business, deals, and politics. George routinely wore golf clothes and we always ate a McDonalds. No nicer people exist and I will miss our talks, George. As George told me, what he does <u>anyone can do on any level.</u>

Jerry J Moore – What a character. A self-made man who specialized in buying, for pennies on the dollar, foreclosed, near vacant community shopping centers in which the grocery story, anchor tenant had gone, leaving struggling "in line" tenants gone or soon to be. Jerry had a cast of regular tenants he'd put into these places, particularly to fill the grocery store space, bringing the center back to life, in short order, just like Onassis did with ships. He left one of the largest private collections of Rolls Royce automobiles ever assembled, 22 collector Ferraris and home of outsized proportion, which matched Jerry's personality. He sold off part of his shopping center portfolio in bulk for $125,000,000.

Darby Suiter

Darby Suiter - Yes, that's Darby playing his saxophone with the dance band he performed with for decades. I first met Darby on a Saturday morning when he came into my office to make a cash offer on a 76 unit apartment in poor condition that I was about to give up on, along with the owner who'd inherited it from his parents. I went on to help Darby expand his portfolio from about 150 to 760 units, all catering to a hugely profitable sub-market of tenants. After selling off his apartment portfolio we were having lunch one day and he asked if I would go look at the last 8 houses he was selling off to get some ideas on marketing them. Only then, after 25 years of friendship, did I find out the full extent of his home investments….150 houses, all kept until they were paid off. He did not need my marketing advice. According to his attorney, he left $50 million in cash and stocks. Except for the tux in this photo, I never saw Darby in much other than jeans, usually working on site alongside his workmen, driving his old truck.

SOME HIGHLIGHTS OF THIS BOOK

Many investors start with homes, but do not understand that they are poor long term investments. True income properties offer greater opportunities for higher rates of returns more safely & simply.

Income properties are actually easy to understand as a few simple keys open the door to endless opportunities to make exceptional returns on investment.

Capitalization, the simple math calculation that assigns a value to the annualized net income, is used the same way on all income property types. This allows for diversification across all manner of real estate investment.

Financial returns from income properties can run for 7% annually to well over 100%, with the bonus on the 100% end of this scale being that you can refinance, keep the cash flow, and recycle one investment over and over, like the convenience store guy was doing.

It's possible to start without cash or credit and earn seed capital, then buy a first income property, then parlay that one into many. It's one way of pursuing the Holy Grail of <u>passive cash flow</u>. But anyone with money to invest can start at step two and accelerate the process.

Approaches to income property investing range from buying market valued properties for good, passive returns (8% to 12% per annum), to gradations of opportunities with increasing returns on investment. It just depends on the temperament and goals of the investor. High returns may require higher risk, but those can be substantially mitigated.

It's possible today to invest nationwide, with a goal of creating, or increasing, passive income, yet still eliminate the need for hands on management on your part.

You now have several ways to pursue these types of investments, actively or passively. You can learn more from my other books & home study course that includes a "get started" monthly series.

SOME FINAL THOUGHTS

What I have summarized for you in this book is the culmination of 39 years in the real estate business. I'm still active too. It's not just my experience either, but the condensed education I received from my many clever clients I've worked with over the years and their years of experience. What's important is that I have put together the best features of what I learned in the residential investing business, which is more experimental than the commercial business I discovered, then applied these concepts to the commercial real estate world. You can now operate in both worlds. But by having an understanding of both residential and commercial properties, a far bigger arena of opportunity is opened for you.

With technology as it is today, one can now invest at a distance too. You are no longer constrained to working out your own back door, though I always encourage people to not assume there are no deals there. Find out first. But the advent of Google Maps, as an example, allows you to put in an address of a property, then "drive" the neighborhood from your computer. With things like Skype, you can talk to and oversee detailed goings on at properties you may hold 1,500 miles away, like my neighbor does with properties he's rehabbing on the east coast while he's here in the mountain west.

To further your education, and you do need to know more than what's in this book, my free email series and other books and home study course will get you what you need. In addition, with my free email series (at www.CashCowRealtyAcademy.com) I'll introduce you to more details and to other experts and mentors I've learned from to provide additional training in all the ideas you've learned about here.

Finally, know that there is <u>no ladder one must climb or dues to pay first</u>. There is no need to do 10 house deals before you look at apartments or strip centers. You are your own boss and no one can tell you how it has to be done. It's an open road with no speed limit. Here's to your success!

MY RELUCTANT START IN REAL ESTATE INVESTING

My real estate investing career began while wandering in a book store. Looking around in the real estate investing section I came across a book by Ron Legrand. A former auto mechanic, Ron had attended a get-rich-in-real-estate-with-no-money-down seminar, paying for the class with borrowed money. A few years later he owned almost 500 homes. During a slowdown in the economy in the 1980's, his empire about buried him when the rent income from all those homes slowed to a trickle. It took him 5 years to unwind the mess. Vowing to never deal with a bank again or take that kind of risk, he devised 4 key ways of making money with houses. I took one of them to heart; lease options.

Now, remember, I knew a lot about big time real estate having already brokered every type of income property for years; office buildings, apartments, shopping centers, etc. Most real estate agents, by the way, never become investors I've noticed.

But following some very broad steps Ron suggested in the book, then finding a promising deal, and signing a document for myself, not as a broker, but as an investor….well, let me just say it was like that first flight with an instructor. Trying to keep my hands off the wheel (yoke), hands in my lap, then steering the plane with my feet was a bit unfamiliar and very uncomfortable. And these were only house deals, but that seemed very daunting.

I'd found an ad in the paper for a vacant home that I came to learn was owned by a recently widowed woman who was now living out of state. It was in an odd location, far from any normal subdivision of similar homes. It was on 3 acres in a subdivision that was only slightly complete but one could keep horses there.

That appealed to a very small market. I think I went out there once, got some pictures, petted some neighboring horses and, all the while, was wondering what I was doing out looking at this house with the wind blowing across the plains, in sight of nothing of distinction. I should be doing big time real estate deals back at the office.

With little more than a contract to buy the place between me and the owner, I find out she's 4 months behind on payments and about to lose it to foreclosure. There's also a second lien on the home from a not-to-happy builder who'd built the home but had not been fully paid; $18,000 was due him.

So, with nothing but a sad widow, an irate builder wanting his money, an unmovable first lien mortgage lender who wanted all their money or they'd foreclose, and a signed contract, I got started ! I put an ad in the paper and some pictures on crude web site. In about two weeks, I got a call from a couple who liked the home from the pictures. She was in Washington DC and her husband was in….Albania ! Well, this is really coming together smoothly. A widow in Oregon, a lender located who knows where, an upset builder, and my buyers; the wife 1,500 miles from this house and the husband somewhere just this side of Jupiter. How was I ever going to extract money from this rats' nest?

Well, it seems Mr. Jupiter was retiring and he and his wife had once lived in this area. Who knew, right ? We went to contract. I negotiated the builder down to accepting $10,000 and we eventually closed both deals the same day; my purchase from Ms. Oregon, using Mr. and Mrs. Jupiter's money and then their purchase from me. They flew in to town and saw the home for the first time the same week they closed on it. I spent no money on anything except pictures, a classified ad, and the web site and when the dust settled I walked away with $8,500. I had maybe 8 hours total time in this whole deal. Widgets for sale ! Yes, I did not get around to doing a lease option, just an assignment of what I'd set up, almost by accident. But the key was a motivated seller.

Now, absorb that if you will. I didn't have specialized knowledge but only an outline of what may be possible. I stumbled through and, with a little luck (Mr & Mrs Jupiter finding this home at the right time), made more money in a few hours than most people make in a month of 40 hour work weeks. You can learn to do this with a lot more than homes as you've seen. In short, anyone willing to learn can do this.

APPENDIX

As you now know, you don't have to own a property in order to make money with it. You can control a property for a limited time with an option agreement or a letter of intent or a contract. You can then control and make use of a property for longer periods by leasing it, a master lease, or having the seller take back a mortgage. All these are methods available to you before you get a loan to fully own a property. One of the best ways to control a commercial property, in fact it's routine with offers on commercial properties, is to start with a letter of intent. I've modified my own to include a 2 week "preliminary" inspection period before the typical 30 day "free look" period in the standard letter of intent begins and a contract is prepared down the road. One can even extend the letter of intent, in writing. I've controlled multi-million properties for months with a letter like this and extensions to it. Here's what one looks like. I came up with the "preliminary inspection period" idea to allow me to get the financial information up front, before proceeding to a contract. It also buys a little more time, s for the standard "due diligence" period to be included in the anticipated contract itself. 30 days for due diligence inspections and, concurrently, 45 days for any third party financing contingency is typical, but not cast in concrete.

SAMPLE LETTER OF INTENT

March 19, 2015

To: Bill Smith - Academy Real Estate

RE: Letter of Intent to Purchase: 2428 50th St – San Antonio, TX
    An Appx 34,177 SF Office Building

Bill, please let this letter serve as an expression of our interest in purchasing the subject property.

BUYER: Southwest Property Trust, Inc via a New LLC to be formed.

PROPOSAL 1

PURCHASE PRICE: $ 1,300,000
TERMS OF PURCHASE: Cash

PROPOSAL 2

PURCHASE PRICE $ 1,375,000
TERMS OF PURCHASE: $ 1,100,000 CASH from Proceeds of a $ 900,000 New First Mortgage obtained by the buyer plus $ 200,000 cash from the buyer, and seller to carry back a second lien mortgage secured by the property the amount of $275,000 at 7% interest only, paid monthly, for 5 years at which time the balance shall be fully due and payable (balloon). If there is currently debt on the property, the $900,000 new first mortgage proceeds will be used to pay the debt off, with any remainder going to the seller.

PRELIMINARY INSPECTION:
Buyer shall have 15 business days from the date this letter of intent is mutually signed to make an initial inspection of the property and review any reasonably requested income and expense information. This information shall include: 2 full years P&L and current year-to-date P&L, appx loan balance and summary of any other liens known to seller, and rent roll. Upon buyers' satisfactory preliminary review, the contract shall be drafted by the purchaser and it will be the intent of the parties to complete it within 5 business days. The purpose of this preliminary inspection is to reduce the time required by a formal contract, so as not to tie the property up for a lengthy time.

CONTRACT INSPECTION PERIOD: The contract shall provide that the buyer, at his sole discretion, shall be allowed 30 calendar days from opening of escrow to review all documentation, obtain third-party reports, and otherwise approve the property. If Buyer determines that, for any reason, the Property is not suitable for Buyer's use, Buyer's earnest money and any additional funds deposited into escrow by Buyer shall be returned to the Buyer within three (3) business days and neither party shall have any liability or obligation to one another hereunder.

FINANCING PERIOD: The contract shall call for a 30 day period from the date a mutually signed contract is receipted by the title company for buyer to secure an interim mortgage loan. This period shall run concurrently with the 30 day inspection period. If the 30th day is a weekend or holiday, the next business day following will be the 30th day.

CONTINUED

EARNEST MONEY DEPOSIT: $ 10,000 – paid upon the expiration of the contract inspection & loan contingency period. The earnest money shall be refundable in the event that the seller is unable to provide related documents or buyer rejection due to inspection period or new first mortgage loan cannot be obtained.

SUGGESTED CLOSING DATE: On or before May 20, 2015

TITLE COMPANY: Fidelity National Title Company- National Commercial Division – Phoenix.

CONFIDENTIALITY: All aspects of this negotiated agreement shall be held by Buyer and Seller and sellers agent in the strictest of confidence until closing.

PRORATION; Taxes, rents, and other income and expenses pertaining to the Property will be prorated as part of the close of escrow.

BROKER DISCLOSURE:
F. Scott Tonges (Southwest Property Trust) is a licensed real estate broker in Colorado and acting as principle for his own account and not involved in any commissions.

SELLER'S OBLIGATION:
The Seller shall provide financial documentation to verify, as applicable, the items listed in the "preliminary inspection" paragraph (above) within six (6) calendar days after the signing of this LOI. The Buyer will pay for appraisal, property inspections, survey, and customary closing costs.

SCOPE OF THIS LETTER:
The Buyer and Seller acknowledge that this proposal is not a legally-binding offer and that it is Intended only as the basis for the negotiations of a purchase contract, nor shall there be any binding Agreement between the parties unless and until a fully executed purchase contract is concluded.

Should the foregoing proposal be acceptable to both parties, a purchase contract will be drafted for both parties review and approval as noted above after preliminary inspection. Upon mutual acceptance of this letter of intent, the Seller agrees to discontinue any third-party sale negotiations. **This proposal shall expire Wednesday, March 25, 2015 at 5 PM, MDT.**

Sincerely,

F. Scott Tonges
President, Southwest Property Trust, Inc / PURCHASER

Approved

_____   _____
Seller   - Signature /Position   Date

_____
Printed Name   Selling Entity

NOTICE: Seller may see buyers background information and letters from prior clients and owners of prior managed properties at www.xxx.com (then to "Bio & Letters" tab at top of screen)
(YOUR CONTACT PHONES, ETC)

ALWAYS GET LEGAL ADVICE ON FORMS & CONTRACTS YOU PLAN TO USE

GETTING STARTED

By reading my other books, getting the free email series, and learning from the complete home study course, you'll learn a lot more about specific property types and more about putting deals together. You'll also learn numerous low or no down payment techniques. But here I'll outline some steps you may wish to take to learn more about the opportunities out there.

Select a Property Type (s) & Size Range

Decide on a City-Town

Select An Area within the City in Which to Focus - Target Area

Get the Address of All The Properties in your Target Area and/or…

Drive the area & Photograph the Properties* and get addresses

Make a list of tenants in the area of your property type with addresses, if commercial.

Look up "For Lease" and "For Sale" Properties in the Target Area (www.loopnet.com)

Get Ownerships of All Properties in Your Target Area

Contact Current Owners in your Target Area

Communicate with them regularly (Letter, post card, newsletter & calls)

Look for Troubled Properties by Seeking Defaulted Loans

Mail Owners a Letter of Your Interest in Buying Properties Like Theirs

Gather the info from the owner

Make Offers

Put Deals Together

SOUTHWEST PROPERTY TRUST INC.
www.SouthwestTrust.com

F. Scott Tonges – President – Southwest Property Trust, Inc

Named among the top 25 commercial real estate brokers in the U.S. during his 8 years with the nation's largest commercial brokerage firm (now CBRE – CB Richard Ellis) out of 1200 agents, Scott began his commercial real estate career in 1976. He has been involved in brokering real estate transactions involving every type of commercial income property: office buildings, shopping centers, apartments, medical buildings, industrial properties, and both full and limited service hotels. He spent one of his 7 years with CBRE (then Coldwell Banker Commercial) as vice president and regional director of apartment property marketing and was responsible for the training and activity of apartment investment brokers in Houston, Dallas, Miami-Ft Lauderdale, Atlanta, & Chicago.

In 1983, as CEO of Polestar Corp. he developed a 5-building, $3.2 million office building project in Houston. In 1985, during the Houston oil down turn, Scott founded his own firm, Tonges-McKelvy. The firm was devoted to commercial and apartment property management. It grew from 2 persons to 100 employees between 1985 thru 1990. The firm managed 554, 507 SF of commercial properties and 1,867 units of apartments in 5 cities – Austin, Houston, Las Vegas, Dallas & San Francisco. Their clients included Texas Commerce Bank, Connecticut Mutual Life Insurance Co, Apple Bank for Savings (New York). In addition to management, the firm oversaw development of a Burger King and a Savings & Loan building for CB Institutional Fund and Friendswood Savings, respectively. He has exclusively represented many private investors and institutional investors in commercial transactions including the commercial real estate investment divisions of Deutsch Bank, Imperial Bank Canada, & Merrill Lynch-Hubbard. This included direct sales, investments, and REO properties. He was regional director of acquisitions for R&B, a Los Angeles based private firm with $1 billion in holdings including 22,000 apartments. He has been involved in commercial transactions of every type from small properties up to a $225 million trophy mall.

He later joined Grubb & Ellis, the nations' second largest commercial real estate brokerage firm. He was named as a Senior Associate there. In addition to investment sales in the southwest, he expanded his activity to include lodging property sales and has been involved in transactions across the country.

Today, Scott is involved in private investment, writing books, newsletters, and creating investor & agent training courses on income property investment. His consulting helps active and passive investors develop cash flow portfolios: from advisory to Done-4-U involvement. He's the creator of the CashCowRealtyAcademy.com & teaches a state approved continuing education course for real estate agents on income property investment & analysis.

He & his wife, Betty, have been licensed private pilots for 19 years. He graduated from Trinity University (San Antonio, TX) with a B.S. degree in physics. He worked for NASA & the Jet Propulsion Lab during the Apollo 11 moon landing. He is a licensed real estate broker in Colorado & teaches state approved, for credit courses in real estate investments to brokers. <u>A packet of client letters is available upon request or see them at www.SouthwestTrust.com (then "ABOUT" tab at top)</u>

LEARN MORE AT

www.CashCowRealtyAcademy.com

Other books & training products by Scott Tonges

How to Turn One $ 2500 Investment into $ 500,000 in 3 to 5 Years Leasing Homes

A step by step guide to how I found deals, tenant buyers, marketed the homes and profited without ownership, all from 200 miles away.

Available at Amazon.com

CASH COWS—The Complete Guide to Commercial, Apartment, & Residential Income Properties & the Hidden World of Extreme Profit Investing

A detailed guide to every form of income property type, how to understand them quickly, make offers, inspect them and profit from them. Includes real world examples, stories you'll benefit from, all about loans, & 25 low & no money down methods. 222 Pages. Available at Amazon.com

The Cash Cow Complete Home Study Course

Includes <u>the books above</u>, a 188 page <u>Workbook</u> (only available with the course) & <u>5 CD's in</u> which I take you page by page through the workbook and real world deals for a deeper understanding. Included is a <u>bonus CD,</u> and <u>3 Free Months</u> of the ongoing monthly series to get you started & making progress and money. Go to:

Www.CashCowAcademy.com — then "Home Study" tab

Includes 3 Free Months of the

"Get Started" Training Series. Each includes a

CD/Book/Lesson

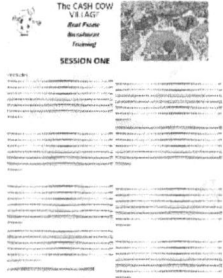

FREE Videos & an Email Series at

www.CashCowRealtyAcademy.com

Here you'll learn more details and ideas about the real world of both commercial and residential investing. I'll also introduce you to some of my mentors and their training as well.

Here's to your success!   F. Scott Tonges